D1240819

MANIFESTATIONS OF THOUGHT

Shah Maghsoud, 1978

MANIFESTATIONS OF THOUGHT

Padidihay-i fikr

Shah Maghsoud Sadiq Angha

Translated with Commentary by

Nahid Angha

International Association of
Sufism Publications

Published by the International Association of Sufism

For more information address:
IAS Publications
PO Box 2382 San Rafael, CA, 94912 USA

Library of Congress Control Number: 2022940011
ISBN: 979-8-9857623-8-9

First published in 1980
Library of Congress Control Number: 81-123489
Educational Testing & Research Institute
San Rafael, California

Cover art, design and typesetting by Susana Marín

Printed and bound in Great Britain
By TJ Books Limited, Padstow, Cornwall

CONTENTS

A NOTE TO THE READER

Many of the references in this book are from works written in Persian, which is a genderless language, while English is a gender-specific language, with masculine and feminine pronouns. Similarly, many words in English are gender exclusive, whereas in Persian the same terms are gender inclusive. Wherever possible, I have translated terms in such a way as to remain gender inclusive (e.g., "human" instead of "man").

All translations are mine unless otherwise noted. Some, including my previously published writings in English, have been further edited for this book.

The intellect of the universe has made it possible for "I" to arrive at this moment of time, on the footsteps of nature in order to claim an identity. This is a great realization that within the vastness of the universe, amid an eternal journey, to me belongs "a space in time."

— Nahid Angha

INTRODUCTION

Padidihay-i fikr, the subject of the present work, written by Shah Maghsoud Sadiq Angha in 1954, Tehran, has eight chapters of philosophical discussions and/or scientific explanations. It is in this book that Shah Maghsoud focuses on the importance of understanding the human being's electromagnetic energies and their relationship with the cosmic energies.

Shah Maghsoud Sadiq Angha (1916 - 1980) was a pre-eminent Iranian Sufi master, poet, and scholar of the Uwaiysi *tariqat* (Sufi order). He formally studied law and political science but devoted much time to exploring Eastern and Western philosophies, mathematics, physics, cosmology, numerology, and literature extensively, thus he was well versed and knowledgeable about Eastern and Western philosophies and mysticism, and his library was abundant with books of many philosophers, spiritual masters and scientific inquirers. A polymath, he remains as one of the prominent Sufi philosophers of the Muslim world. His doctrines address the questions of creation, of the universe, of God, of infinite/finite, of ethics and morality, of existence (*wujud*); of essence and quiddity (*māhiyat*), the relationship of human beings with the greater universe, and so on; and like his predecessors, he employs the most complex and sophisticated language in explaining his doctrines.

· WORKS ·

He wrote his first book *Kukab-i adab* (lit. Star of Literature) in his teen years, and his last, *Diwan-i ghazal* (Book of Sonnet) at 64.

His philosophical and metaphysical works include *Padidihay-i fikr*[1] (lit. Manifestations of Thought), written when he was in his mid-thirties and deeply engaged in scientific and philosophical studies. His *Zavaya-i makhfi-i hayati* (Hidden Angles of Life)[2] focuses on wave energies including cosmological, celestial energies and gravitational forces that surround and affect us in and beyond our galaxy. He writes on the nature of metals, numbers, weights, and balances in his *Ozan va-mizan* (lit. Weights and Balances);[3] and explains the notions of ultimate unity and finite dimensions saturating our universe in his *Hamaseh-i hayat* (lit. The Epic of Life).[4] Shah Maghsoud also writes on the stations of the heart and the lights associated with these stations in this book. *Mathnawi mazamir-i haqq va Golzar-i omid* (lit. Psalms of Truth, and the Garden of Hope)[5] written in prose and poetry, is focused on the science of *jafr* (the numerical symbolism of the letters of the Arabic alphabet). In his *Sahar* (Dawn)[6] he included a short treatise on the reality of the self and Self, humans and God, and and includes a short treatise to the history of Sufism.

He has extended his writings to traditional medicine and devoted a book to that subject called: *Tib-i sunnati* (Traditional Medicine)[7] that gives an overview of the "nature of elements," and their relationship to the four elements (fire, air, water, and earth). His *Sayr al-hajar* (Secret

---

[1] *Padidihay-i fikr* also published in one volume compendium: *Nirvan, Avaz-i-khudayan, Payam-i dil, Padidihay-i fikr* (Tehran: Amin Publications, 1963), trans. Nahid Angha, *Padidihay-i fikr: Manifestations of Thought* (San Rafael, California: Educational Testing & Research Institute, 1980).

[2] Shah Maghsoud Sadiq Angha, *Zavaya-i makhfi-i hayati* (Tehran: Amin Publishers, 1975); the English version was published as *Hidden Angles of Life* (Pomona, California: Multidisciplinary Publications, 1975).

[3] Shah Maghsoud Sadiq Angha, *Ozan va-mizan* (Tehran: Amin Publications, 1975).

[4] Shah Maghsoud Sadiq Angha, *Hamaseh-i-hayat* (Abadan: Journal of the Literary Society of Abadan, 1970; Tehran: Amin Publications, 1974).

[5] Shah Maghsoud Sadiq Angha, *Mathnawi mazamir-i haqq va Golzar-i omid* (Tehran: Kitab-Furushi Zavaar Publications, 1963).

[6] Shah Maghsoud Sadiq Angha, *Sahar* (Tehran: Maktab-e-tariqat-e-Oveyssi Shah Maghsoudi, 1977), trans. Nahid Angha, *Sahar* (San Rafael, California: Educational Testing & Research Institute, 1981).

[7] Shah Maghsoud Sadiq Angha, *Tib-i-sunnati* (Tehran: Maktab-e-tariqat-e-Oveyssi Shah Maghsoudi, 1978).

of the Stone)[8] refers to the science of letters and numbers. Sections of this book had been included in his *Ozan va-mizan.*

In addition to his philosophical and scientific works, Shah Maghsoud devoted several books to mysticism, spiritual journey, meditation, and stages of the heart, including *Avaz-i khudayan* (Psalms of Gods),[9] one of his most beautiful literary works written in the literary style of rhythmic prose, with a puzzling question of "gods" in plural form. He so masterfully explains this plurality where every spiritual traveler, every being, even with his limitations and physical dimensions, is like a "song," a "psalm" praising the divine presence in both its manifestations and essence, in dimensions and in the abstract; where Lordship (*rububiyya*) resides at the very heart of the servanthood (*'ubudiyyat*), as the *hadith* of the Prophet relates.

Another of his acclaimed works is *Chante: Jahan-i 'Arif* (*Chante*: The Universe of the Knower)[10] written in 1946 when Shah Maghsoud was in his late twenties. He answers and explains philosophical, scientific, and spiritual questions and uses the beautiful style of sonnet to explain the journey of the Essence in the language of numerology and cosmology. Another of his poetic masterpieces is *Payam-i dil* (lit. Message of the Heart)[11] that includes instructions and teachings for seekers of a spiritual journey and contains references to his notion of *'uqdah-i hayati*, an exclusive concept that became his signature doctrine. His *Nirvan*[12] is the story of creation, has seven sections, corresponding to the days of the creation story, along with the final day when Nirvan, the aware and enlightened human being, settles in the house of infinity and hears the

---

[8] Shah Maghsoud Sadiq Angha, *Sayr al-hajar* (San Rafael, California: MTO Shahmaghsoudi Publications, 1983).

[9] Shah Maghsoud Sadiq Angha, *Avaz-i khudayan* (Tehran: Amin Publishers, 1963), trans. Nahid Angha, *Psalms of Gods* (California: International Association of Sufism Publications, 1991).

[10] Shah Maghsoud wrote this book in 1946, but it took him until 1962 to complete and publish (Tehran: Misbahi Publisher, 1962; *Chante* was reprinted in Tehran 1965 and 1976 by Behjat Publishers.)

[11] Shah Maghsoud Sadiq Angha, *Payam-i-dil*, trans. Nahid Angha, *A Meditation: Payam-i dil* (San Rafael, California: IAS Publications, 1991).

[12] Shah Maghsoud Sadiq Angha, *Nirvan* (Tehran: Amin Publishers, 1960), trans. Nahid Angha, *Nirvan* (San Rafael, California: International Association of Sufism Publications, 1992; second edition, 2021).

herald of hope echoing within infinite existence declaring that there is no non-existence and that existence is the One and Only.

His *Al-Rasa'il* (lit. Treatises)[13] is a four-section treatise, and one of the sections is dedicated to the Islamic prayer, or *salat* (*namaz* in Persian), wherein Shah Maghsoud analyzes the significance of each element of every prescribed movement. He explains that each movement in the Islamic prayer represents a letter. Each letter has a shape, and the shape of each one of those movements make the alphabetical shape of *la ilaha illa allah*, the declaration of unity in Islam. Shah Maghsoud's *Mathnawi shahid va-mashud* and *Mathnavi seyr-sa'ir va-tayr-i nadir* is a compilation of two manuscripts published in one volume, includes Sufi stories and words of advice, written in the poetic style of a *mathnawi*. *Diwan-i ghazal* (The Book of Sonnets)[14] is Shah Maghsoud's last work. He compiled this book of his sonnets and quatrains in 1979 and dedicated the book to me. I have translated and published selections from this book in my own works as well as in articles and lectures. I included a preface and two pages of his handwritten poems in his published *Diwan*.

· TRANSLATIONS ·

I began translating *Padidihay-i fikr* long ago when I was still a university student. As I began studying this critically acclaimed book, along with Shah Maghsoud's other literatures, I realized the difficulties of translating those mystical and philosophical texts; finding equivalent term and word to deliver similar "meaning" from one language to another; and considering the rhythmic and or poetic language that were imbedded in those tests, I have asked him to set a schedule to guide me through his writings, and doctrines. Those many years of extensive discussions were of great benefit. They helped me not only understand the minutiae of Shah Maghsoud's thoughts but also return to my translations and commentaries with a greater clarity. I compiled

---

[13] Shah Maghsoud Sadiq Angha, *Al-Rasa'il* (Tehran: Maktab-e-tariqat-e-Oveyssi Shah Maghsoudi, 1978).

[14] Shah Maghsoud Sadiq Angha, *Diwan-i ghazal* (San Rafael, California: International Association of Sufism Publications, 1984).

my first commentary of *Padidihay-i fikr* in 1978, and Shah Maghsoud published it as: *Negāh: Tahshi'-i bar Padidihay-i fikr* in 1979, Tehran (with his calligraphy on the cover). The English translation (*Manifestations of Thought*) was published in California in October 1980, together with a short commentary. That translation and commentary have been further edited for this present work.

· COMMENTARY ·

The philosophical theories and doctrines cited in this new commentary are limited to those referred to in the *Padidihay-i fikr* itself. In the last few years, several sections of the translation and/or commentary have been edited for and published in the *Sufism: An Inquiry* Journal; a few sections were edited and included in *Shah Maghsoud: Life and Legacy* (2021).

Shah Maghsoud has addressed several important philosophical and scientific principles and theories in this work; here, I have selected only a few, and mainly from the topics I have discussed in the 1979 Persian language commentary of his *Padidihay-i fikr*.

Shah Maghsoud begins his *Padidihay-i fikr* with these magnificent statements:

> As the sound waves are spread into space by set computations so the susceptible recipient, according to its capacity and power, receives and records the sound waves, so are the effects of human beings' thoughts; they, too, will surely search and find—without time limitation—its suitable receivers within this boundless existence.[15]

And so my deepest gratitude to Shah Maghsoud whose life gave birth to mine; who led me to the *ka'ba* of my heart; who guided me to see the hidden treasure within the heart of the heart.

Nahid Angha
San Rafael, California
October 24, 2022

TRANSLATION

If the introductory words of essential laws were discovered and the secrets of the spoken and living book of self were revealed, then we would be free from the dead and lifeless books and become closer to the richness within.

Mir Ghotbeddin Muhammad[1]

· INTRODUCTION ·

I do not write this treatise to correct a deviant intellectual or to warn a passenger of the road he or she has taken, his/her location and station. My only duty is to present the truths which I have discovered and become acquainted with throughout my life. But if someone should ask my reasons for this presentation, I would say that as sound waves are spread into space by arranged computation, so any susceptible recipient, according to its level of capacity and power, can record the sound. The effects of any individual's thought will surely search and find—without any limitation of time—its suitable receivers within reality.

In these treatises I have to mention my discoveries of reality which are harmonized with my identity. I am not the wisest human being of my time whose words become unchangeable laws. I have no intention to overwhelm the reader's mind with meaningless words that will lead us nowhere. We cannot be proud of memorizing the works of others, since they are not ours. The memorization of what we do not know prevents us from understanding and honoring our own richness within the design of the existence.

At a glance, everyone realizes that even the most logical and reasonable word cannot define the feeling and quality of meaning. It will not transfer the meaning through the ear to the mind, so that the listener

---

[1] Mir Ghotbeddin Muhammad Angha, Shah Maghsoud's father and spiritual teacher, was a Persian Sufi master (1887-1962).

conceives of the same message as the sender. For example, if you say to a thirsty person "water," that person never feels the same sensation as if he or she were to drink water. The word "water" gives only an incomplete notion of a forgotten quality that is never comparable with that truer, more sensible quality of drinking water. In other words, you can never feed and fill a hungry person simply by saying "bread," the word spoken will never produce the same result as giving bread and letting an individual eat.

A careful glance shows us that the very same problem exists with any word that has been said. The problem is more apparent when the speaker is not aware of the words he or she is uttering. There is another problem with words as well: they have no similarity to their defined meaning. For example, when an orator gives a speech, each individual in the audience perceives the words spoken according to his or her own experience. If the audience is not familiar with the speaker's words, then the audience will not understand those spoken words. Since everyone has a very personal way of thinking, perceiving and talking, when two people are speaking together, the only things perceived that make sense are those conceptions which cause agreement. Otherwise, the speaker and listener are two different people who speak different languages and do not understand each other.

René Descartes (French philosopher, d. 1650) observes that a human being learns more through his or her own experiences than from others' experiences.[2] Many times an individual might have a conversation with a philosopher, a scientist, or a mystic; the individual seemed to understand the opinions of those intellectuals [or anyone's, for that matter]. But by the time that individual repeats what they told him or her, he or she will express completely different ideas; so different that one could hardly recognize the original talks.

---

[2] For more information see René Descartes, *Discourse on Method*, trans. Ian Maclean (New York: Oxford University Press, 2008). Originally published in 1637 in French. Also see Gary Hatfield, "René Descartes," *The Stanford Encyclopedia of Philosophy* (Summer 2018 Edition), Edward N. Zalta (ed.), URL = <https://plato.stanford.edu/archives/sum2018/entries/descartes/>. Section 3.1, "How Do Our Minds Know?" summarizes some of the basic tenets of Descartes' thought, and references his views as expressed in his *Principles on Philosophy* and *Meditations and Other Metaphysical Writings*.

Words are made simply as signs for things or known common properties, and people use them to communicate with each other, to expect moral meanings from them is impossible. If an individual tries to study words and make them the basis for improving his mind, and training his essential understanding, he or she is just exhausting his or her memory and binding his or her curious mind by illogical logic!

Gottfried Wilhelm Leibniz (German philosopher, d. 1716) identifies that when the qualities of a thing, for which we only have a verbal description, lead to an understanding of it, we cannot be certain of the accuracy of the definition. Descriptions may mislead us; therefore, truths by themselves are not related to words.[3]

I have no intention of making void the verbal agreements and conventions which rule among people, but what I mean to say is that no one perceives meaning only through words, unless one has experienced these meanings in the depth of one's own essential being, or spirituality.

The only time we perceive perfect meaning in the word we hear is when we happen to be in the reality of that perfection; and then we know that the meaning of every word exists in its reality and will not be displaced from its true place by the word.

If it is acceptable that purity of spirit [the very essence of one's being] is the basis and principle for conceiving meaning, then nothing is more valuable than studying the spirit [flow of life-energy] which is the purpose of existence.

My suggestion is that instead of spending our most valuable time studying books that lead us nowhere, we must strive within our "self" to become acquainted with our own reality; to make our brains a capable recipient to receive the sublime moral waves from those thoughtful minds who precede us.

Since acquaintance with truth will not be acquired by reasoning, I expect the reader to examine my interpretations away from the limitations of imperfect sensations in order to analyze the words and statements. One may then cooperate with future readers and investigators of this book to complete the message. My great master, my father, protected

---

[3] For more information see G.W. Leibniz, *New Essays on Human Understanding*, trans. Peter Remnant and Jonathan Bennett (United Kingdom: Cambridge University Press, 1996). Originally published in 1765.

my child-like mind with his moral teachings. Since his teachings were far from selfish or ambitious, my mind has not accepted any other way of thought. If these writings lead on the road of civilization, then I am happy; otherwise, how can we be proud of what we do not accomplish?

Sadiq Angha
February 1954
Tehran

The past scientific discoveries are but introductory works to future understanding; the reality of knowledge is but founded upon consciousness and the essence of human self.

If we considered the minds of the scientists as the extremity of knowledge, final scientific and philosophical hypotheses would have been reached and the certainty and truth about nature should have been announced by now. However, since a scientist sets his or her thought in the essence of his or her own being, and believes in a stable centrality within the 'self,' a centrality that is infinite, then he or she can travel through a 360-degree circumference surrounding, through a progressive computation on the table of the existence. Though this scientist will never get to the edge and boundary of this surrounding, wherever he or she is, he or she conceives of peace and tranquility resulting from the truth of nature and the nature of truth. Therefore, this individual will not be misled by comparing appearance, and will not take appearances as facts. The privilege of tranquility and contentment is that no scientist will be amazed with his or her hypothesis as if it were a great surprise to the world. He or she looks at his or her hypothesis as an introduction to knowledge.

If we take a look at the astronomers' ideas, or announcements made by astronomical observatories about planets, galaxies and so forth, they may suggest that there are other planets, with inhabitants probably more sophisticated than us, who might have taken greater steps in their advancements and made use of electrodynamics, atomic energy, mirror image, or some other finding which we do not know about; even that they have overcome the darkness of nights on their planet. Comparing the intensity of electricity and magnetic energies in Mars with our own planet might be like comparing medieval lamps with modern lights. This example, and many others, may help the beginner in scientific research to look at scientific theories, thoughts and findings as the introduction to science, not the finality of them. If we use simple thoughts, and grow tired of researching a subject thoroughly, we may not understand that even the newest method in any scientific hypothesis is not the finality of existence. The conception of a scientific point is one of the countless conceptual areas that coincide with the very potentiality of the scientist's mind in his continual search for perfection. Therefore, it is not Isaac Newton's or Galileo's eyes conceiving actions and reactions, but their stable and focused character which acquaints them with the gravity or rotation of the earth. (They even extended their knowledge of appearances to reality.)[4]

A less sophisticated and knowledgeable human being, whose character is forgotten and scattered, lost, and dispersed in the levels of natural reactions and appearances, is always astounded by general appearances and may not remain focused on a stable point. This person sees all natural appearances and scientific discoveries as so unchangeable that in order to use them, he must refer to those written, planned methods which have been used before. Since the basis of inquiry and initiation are silent, dead in his or her mind, he or she has grown more obedient, imitative and adaptive in his or her thoughts and actions. This individual thinks, for example, that a computer could not have been anything else or used differently from what it is now. Such individuals are always extraneous to the scientific community since they fail to make use of scientific research and advancements. This kind of human could never give an idea dignity or open his or her nature to inquire. He or she is satisfied with what nature has necessarily given him or her.

Insensitive minds mistake essential truths for introductions. They behave like a child who has learned the alphabet and repeats it loudly

---

[4] Isaac Newton (English mathematician and physicist, d. 1727) made discoveries across the fields of mathematics, mechanics, optics, and astronomy that became the basis of understanding across these disciplines. His three laws of motion, the basic principles of modern physics, resulted in the formulation of the law of universal gravitation. Newton's *Mathematical Principles of Natural Philosophy* is considered one of the greatest scientific works in human history. See Andrew Janiak, "Newton's Philosophy," *The Stanford Encyclopedia of Philosophy* (Winter 2019 Edition), Edward N. Zalta (ed.), URL = <https://plato.stanford.edu/archives/win2019/entries/newton-philosophy/>. Galileo Galilei (Italian physicist, d. 1642) is credited with developing the experimental scientific method, and made fundamental contributions to the sciences of motion, mechanics and astronomy. His discoveries with the telescope supported a heliocentric understanding of the solar system in which the Earth and other planets revolve around the Sun. See Peter Machamer and David Marshall Miller, "Galileo Galilei," *The Stanford Encyclopedia of Philosophy* (Summer 2021 Edition), Edward N. Zalta (ed.), URL = <https://plato.stanford.edu/archives/sum2021/entries/galileo/>.

to show everyone that he or she has conceived of something new. They may even think that no one has learned this truth before, and that such truth has not been previously discovered. I remember a child who saw a book of natural science for the first time and then asked me if I had read one and knew what it was. He asked me in a way to make me understand what a learned fellow he was. But he never thought that studying the introduction was just the beginning of a discipline. After studying a few introductions to some science and learning a few laws, this child will treat some, or even all, of his mind's gatherings as unchangeable and fixed laws.

This method of thought is like an attorney's defense against a client's charges, which should be according to and limited by the court's laws. In other words, all of the attorney's defense should be applicable to the law. The attorney's thoughts are not permitted to go beyond those written and planned laws. The only thing he or she can do is to explain the laws as a defense. The beginners are bound by past knowledge and when they want to represent themselves or accept an investigation, their standards of acceptance are those old written formulas.

But if some day the beginner's mind matures and attains more capacity to conceive of new or even sudden clues, and he or she asks the reason for his or her investigation into the past, his or her conscious mind may assure that he or she has studied the past to understand the future. But if the future is just another review of the past, it is naive and unscientific. An individual who talks about a scientific idea is not a scientist him or herself. And a person who reads Hafiz's poems in a very fine tone does not have the spiritual and essential privilege of Hafiz.[5]

I have seen many people who have memorized the words or works of great individuals and represented them to an audience with such pride, as if they have done something important. They may not even realized that what they have done is nothing but memorizing the past. Still water stored in a sink will never be more wholesome than running water. The wealth of one's memory, even if the details are recited, is not

---

[5] Shams-ud din Muhammad Ḥafiz of Shiraz (d. 1390) was a Persian poet, whose collected works, especially *ghazal* (sonnet) are regarded as great masterpieces of Persian literature.

more than a library. But a thoughtful inquiry into past learning shows and represents lively movement in its investigator's nature. This kind of searching mind is expected to find scientific and moral results in the future. We can refer to this vital innate motive as "inspiration" and or "revelation." It is when one is inspired when one's whole character conforms and coincides with a perception, understands beyond comparison. We should treat revelation, which is a deep and true acquaintance within essential existence, as the higher level of inspiration and insight. Those newly introduced to these levels have no knowledge of past thought; and, as a matter of fact, their only connection with them is in general information. For example, if a scientific theory confirms some theories and denies others, it must be treated as a comparison between past and present, because this new theory has not been intentionally constituted in order to confirm or deny previous thoughts. It has happened because a researcher, in his or her comparative studies was led to these new confirmations and denials; and, this scientific theory has its own details, independent and apart from other theories.[6]

Henri Bergson (French philosopher, d. 1941) establishes that the masterpiece of a writer or the acting of an actor in a scene will never give the audience true knowledge about the character in the story. An audience will not receive or become acquainted with the reality and actuality of the character only by reading the book or seeing the play.[7] The absence of actual conditions, plus the unreal and dissimilar comparison between the writer's mind and that of the actor's, lead to a false evaluation of the character. This lack of coincidence proves what Bergson asserts. It is obvious that some things are relatively acceptable and some are not. Since independence of thought is certain, knowledge, whether or not it is metaphoric or real, should be far beyond necessary sense considerations and relative comparative repetitions because these considerations are not new. They are a repeated study and even with an exact assumption in the mind of the observer, it may not be similar to the way which we may take and follow in the future.

---

[6] Even though those past theories might have served as foundations for new studies, but we have to recognize each study independently.

[7] See Henri Bergson, *Creative Evolution* (New York: Henry Holt and Company, 1911). Also see *Henry Bergson Key Writings*, ed. Keith Ansell Pearson and John Mullarkey (first published: New York: Continuum, 2002).

There is also something else to note. Sensory contact, which some believe is the basis of sensory sciences, is faced with some limitations. That is, one cannot get to know a character in a story through his or her own observation, and it will not lead one to that true cognition as the character of the story has of him or herself. If there were a play called *Socrates*, written by Plato, that was brought to the stage and introduced to the audience, the real Socrates would remain unknown; the Socrates in the play is made up. In other words, what we get to know through the perfect acting of an actor is not the real Socrates, but one who is created with no similarity to that Greek philosopher Socrates. Socrates is a real being and none of his life details can be brought to the stage accurately. Socrates, whose character speaks truth and does whatever suits him, is not the same individual described by Plato or played on the stage by an actor. The character Socrates was as it was, and when Plato tried to introduce and describe Socrates, he actually introduced and described himself.

Those principles which are perceived by nature and proved by the intellect are considered to be factual knowledge and therefore original. Observations which are based on natural, sensory comparisons are not stable truths and do not even possess essentiality. Such observations are in an imaginary position and in the dark, so they should not be confused with actual knowledge, or *'irfan*.

In *The Great Secret*, Maurice Maeterlinck (Belgian playwright and poet, d. 1949) explained his sensory perception with a family who was gathering and carrying crops in the distance.[8] While the truth of that picture with its fine overall use of color seemed appreciable and was glowing in the viewer's eyes, it was, at the same time, carrying joyful, sad, hard, and painful private memories. Its reality appeared in such a way that suits the viewer's sensory encounters and apprehensions, but the qualities of the surface itself were hidden from his eyes.

This very careful discussion, which has some important psychological ramifications, shows us clearly that sensory observations are conducted and regulated according to the observer's mental acceptance. Therefore, conceptions resulting from external images are just descriptions of

---

[8] See Maurice Maeterlinck, *The Great Secret*, trans. Bernard Miall (first published: New York: The Century co., 1922).

the observer's momentary state of mind and mood. This knowledge is based on physical appearances, and the way they are apprehended by the observer, and not on the reality of the scenery and observed objects. For example, an attractive lawn or a green, lively garden with a fixed appearance in a point of time gives different apprehensions and feelings to, for instance, a man sentenced to death, who has one hour to live; a prisoner who had a lifetime conviction; a poet who is busy with his emotions, motivations and feelings; or a child. Sometimes these conceptual qualities are so different from and opposite to each other that their subjective images may be represented by two or more different pictures; but, as we know, there is just one observed sensory picture giving different impressions.

A sensory observation will usually recall memories in the conscious mind and is contributed to and accompanied by the association of ideas that will color the observer's view. Since human identity [one's self-hood] and mental acceptance interfere with physical appearances of real consequences and indications, it is likely to say that it is impossible to conceive of objects as they are. Therefore, external, superficial observations, which conscience [the mind] photographs and analyzes according to its present qualities, are unreal and made up and shall not be called knowledge.

It has been mentioned before that factual knowledge is free from any comparisons, relations and redundancies, and is conceived of as consciousness. It searches for and looks at metaphysics, and beyond, for its concepts. Thus, it is called concrete knowledge and when it corresponds with and conforms to sense-pictures, it should be known as acquirements [something gathered by the senses].

Existence is sentenced to its own destiny, freewill of the limited and dimensional pieces of such infinite universe are, too, drawn into the infinite circles of destiny.

The representation of sunlight to the Earth in the infinite universe shows that there is an invisible and unknown ray that can only be observed on the starting and destination of the light wave. In other words, the Earth's daytime, with all its usual activities and businesses, looks like any other planet to the eyes of the inhabitants of the other planets. The light waves contact the atmosphere around the planet so as to make light and bright reactions visible on the surface of the Earth or any planet.

In this infinite orbit, the magnetic wave controls the setting and destiny of orbital arrangement, and nowhere has been left out of these strong, influential dynamics. Yet, when we look at the planets, satellites and halos in the Milky Way, they seem to be working independently, without any connections or transactions with each other.

In this universe in the orbital atmosphere roaring and transacted waves lead lost, wandering and undecided enormous planets and galaxies to their destinations. They compute and manage the universe with a very careful arrangement, even as they seem so silent and quiet, and the sky looks as though it has nothing to do at all. But if a simple little substance, or atom, moves and displaces from its axis unexpectedly, it will take the whole universe to an unknown destination so that the existence of nature, as it is now, will be in doubt.

These are factual, yet poetic, thoughts suited to be perceived by human sensory perception and comprehension. However, there are still so many surprises and mysteries within nature that are not known, as yet, to human beings. But how can these arranged and computed natural appearances and happenings make sense to an earthly being like us? It is impossible for me to accept the idea that total orbital disciplines and systems have no influence on the way I live my life, the way I think, or on my being as a whole. It is unacceptable to agree that a creature who comes into being from Nature's womb, and who has been cherished by and existed because of Nature's necessary entity (whose monumental and present being is the result of a long voyage), will defy or neglect natural laws in order to control Nature and ignores the governing principles.

Nature is a capable master that does not violate or defy the continuous and successive stages of eternal destiny. Even imaginable accidents and obstacles cannot change its direction. Nature leads its hypothetical members so freely and with such authority in a specific direction that there is no choice left to any being. But when a human being uses the ability and prestige given to him or her by Nature, without realizing that he or she is being controlled by its determinate constraints, he or she imagines that he or she is free in thought and will, and that Nature has respected and given him or her a unique quality which Nature probably does not even own. Logical reasoning, however, can easily refute this misunderstanding.

Descartes, for example, introduced his idea of a vacuum in 1631.[9] That scientific investigation was continued in experiments with a glass pipe of mercury in 1643 as Evangelista Torricelli (Italian physicist, d. 1647), using these ideas, explained air pressure by calculating the weight of 76 centimeters of height on one square centimeter of mercury.[10] According to this finding, from the very moment materials arrive at corporal form they adjust to this pressure; and this is one of nature's forces on all beings-humans, animals, etc. They all have to obey this law. This natural effect, which is one of the smallest governors and leaders in human life, has complete influence on human being's wellbeing. Though this effect is observable and, imagining such a pressure is frightening, yet human being is not thinking about such a natural force, even for a moment, in his or her lifetime. Yet, from the moment of birth, human being has to obey this natural constraint without even knowing it. If you think of the moon for a second, as an example, you will see that, although the moon is almost the smallest planet in orbit and follows the Earth in every action and direction, it has a great influence on the Earth. The

---

[9] See Daniel Gerber, *Descartes' Metaphysical Physics* (Chicago: University of Chicago Press, 1992) 127–130.

[10] See Frederick John Jervis-Smith, *Evangelista Torricelli* (first published: Oxford: Oxford University Press, 1908) 15–17.

moon's rotations, or revolutions and movements, as we know, have great effects on oceans and seas. Since in the infinite circular orbit the Earth and its inhabitants are affected by these conditions, beyond our control or understanding, how would we expect not to be influenced and controlled physically or mentally, by such determined systems which suit a human being's destination?

How is the human being, a finite being, an almost nonexistent body, compares itself with the infinite universe, and even claims possessing a free will? The reflections of orbital gravitations on capable and susceptible minds, though they may not be visible, are not less influential than the influence of gravitations or invisible waves on luminous planets, as the Sun is to the Earth.

If hearing were more stable and capable of perceiving more accurately, we could follow the directions of sublime thoughts in the depth of Newton's and Kepler's sky, just as we can follow the orbital gravitations.[11] Their validity is expected to be related to something other than the natural existence of the Earth and is a result of a general rational system. If the orbital gravitations lead the orbital planets, why can't an orbital rationale lead the planets' inhabitants to sacredness?

When the intellectual findings, in a moment, introduce one of the natural mysteries to a susceptible mind, as soon as the proportionality in the physical and spiritual [intrinsic and essential] system of the mind with an overall susceptibility of the brain system comes into being, physical and metaphysical waves cause a special influence on the third passage of the intellect (mind), which is the descending place of these waves. Then the sensitive senses of the thinker cut the unreal distances caused by sensory contacts. Through the observations of natural reality and its coincidence with human intrinsic and essential inherit potentiality an individual will discover a theoretical or essential principle. And because of a factual concurrence, human being approves of the reality of that principle in the depth of his or her heart and confirms it with his conscience and conscious mind. Of course, it is obvious

---

[11] Johannes Kepler (German mathematician and astronomer, d. 1630) is best known for his laws of planetary motion. See Daniel A. Di Liscia, "Johannes Kepler," *The Stanford Encyclopedia of Philosophy* (Fall 2019 Edition), Edward N. Zalta (ed.), URL = https://plato.stanford.edu/archives/fall2019/entries/kepler/.

that the stability of physical or intrinsic laws is related to the element of coincidence between a person's factual character and existential levels. As a matter of fact, the closer our physical and sensory systems remain in harmony with the governing principles of the nature, the more confidence they should reach. To comprehend any concept in which its elementary effect is observable in nature, the first step is to explore the subject, break down its limitations and restrictions, and notice the way it is related, attached and transacted with the infinite; otherwise, none of the natural, sensory observations are enough to clear a truth, and such a deep final observation is not possible through one individual sense.

In *Extra-Sensory Perception*, Joseph Banks Rhine (American para-psychologist, d. 1980) identified cognition as the ability to conceive of magnetic rays or waves that come to us from objects surrounding us.[12] These waves pass through all materials and objects without need of a natural substance. Rhine distinguishes that a clear-sighted human being is the one who has control over a part of his or her brain and can conceive the rays from a certain point.[13] Such an individual's action is like the wireless receiver. It sorts out the undesirable waves and receives only the harmonious, appointed and desired wave.[14]

As a matter of fact, Newton's law of universal gravitation, which says that the force of gravitational attractions between two bodies is equal to the product of the mass of the two bodies divided by the square of their distance apart, is just the introductory principle to the natural transactions, which of course, is not what we discuss here.[15]

Animal magnetism has qualities and disciplines that we will discuss

---

[12] See J.B. Rhine, *Extra-Sensory Perception* (Boston: B. Humphries, 1964).

[13] Ibid.

[14] When an individual learns to collect and concentrate one's electro and magnetic energies in a point of reference (in Sufism that point of reference is the heart), one will create an atmosphere or environment of electro and magnetic energies that is open to harmonious waves only. Thus realization, discovery, inspiration and revelation are the results of human being's collection, concentration and focus of energies in a point of reference (brain/mind or heart/spirit). This principle has become the fundamental principle in Shah Maghsoud's practice of meditation.

[15] See Isaac Newton, *The Principia: Mathematical Principles of Natural Philosophy*, trans. I. Bernard Cohen and Anne Whitman (Berkeley: University of California Press, 1999).

16

later. When Joseph Rhine suggests that a clear-sighted human must have control over a part of his brain in order to receive magnetic waves, he probably means the coincidence and coordination between corporeal and non-corporeal hidden ability and the universal dynamics, which we have mentioned before. This makes the human brain susceptible to receive any special electromagnetic waves.

However, careful scientific investigation have basic introductions and records and have gradually completed and changed scientific developments for human society. These discoveries have been perceived and examined first in the brains of scientists; but no doubt the dominant agent in these discoveries is the universe. It is obvious that essential fundamentals, or conditions, are needed for both sender and receiver systems to cooperate. For example, if some sound waves are broadcast on a special wavelength, a receiver will receive the waves on a channel; but these sound waves are of no use to a receiver that is not equipped to receive nor is in harmony with those waves, though these broadcast waves are distributed over space and surround the Earth's atmosphere. This approximate example and qualitative picture is comparable to any scientific transaction and activity. Our orbit is full of physical and metaphysical happenings, but our knowledge about them is insignificant. Our physical and mental system of knowledge is far too limited to understand the way things happen, are inspired and discovered.

The first step to perceive and comprehend a meaning or a concept is the realization that the concept and the conceiver must be on the same electro-magnetic wave-level and in harmony with all existent conditions. For example, we cannot conceive of sound or light waves that have frequencies above or below our ability to hear and see. What we perceive is related to our present being, and the results we gather are merely comparisons and proportions that contrast with, and are basically different from, universal principles.

Eastern clear-sighted and intuitive scientists believe that if all of a human being's natural powers and strengths, senses, sensory perceptions, or other mental faculties, can be concentrated on a precise, sensitive, metaphysical point of existence—or become accustomed to comprehending truth and reality, superior to sense limitations and animal habits—they can then cognize more clearly and precisely natural principles that have metaphysical terms, because the sum total of a few strengths is more powerful than those strengths individually.

When an individual reaches this concentration [or, as a matter of fact, when the strength of organized existence harmonizes with the will of the intellect or the rationale], then any precise manifestations and picture reflects on that individual's clear, susceptible conscience (mind/heart). He or she will then be able to comprehend and recognize even the energies beyond waves—those which he or she is not familiar with—and he or she will be able to comprehend the spirit and divinity of him or herself and those materials in the depth of his or her mind and soul. Intuition and cognition mean that one should not mistake superficiality for reality, but should intuit things as they are. Therefore, when leading a character or individual to the greater strengths and energies of nature, brain faculty and sense perception should coincide and correspond with conditions and circumstances. This quality is spiritual and a positive step for intelligent people (minds, selves, characters) and their souls; those are the ones that nature introduces once in a while as perfect examples of learned wise individuals.

Fragmented natural energies result in the loss of sensory exactness, because like a machine whose parts work individually and differently, they become useless. Those who are unaware of their innate essential understanding and knowledge remain improvident and their manner and deed could not become laws for human principles.

An honorable society is a responsible society; and a responsible society aims to improve scientific developments and provide education for its members; and inspires its scholars and knowledgeable individuals.

When orbital, infinite organized gravitational forces, according to the reality of time, infuse their intersection of rays in a sensitive or thoughtful brain cell and lead a mind to discover one of nature's mysteries or open a new way to humanity's present and future civilization, a hypothesis from that trivial, scientific incident will present itself, and that will lead towards new and experimental sciences. If true and real susceptibility is present, the expression and issuing of that incident comes into being as well. Although the scientific incident may appear to be insignificant at the beginning, in a short time it will obtain an international, scientific status and will be used globally.

We should not forget that if those introductory grounds were not supported and protected by other necessary materials and means, the time they present themselves would be delayed or even lost. There have been many excellent ideas and complex thoughts, which were like the sun behind clouds and fire behind ashes, hidden in the dark corners of ordinary human societies waiting to express themselves; but, they stayed and remained in cold despair and a hopeless surrounding—in the thoughts of the thinker and in the mind of the discoverer until they were forgotten and given away to the ultra-waves to travel along their arc-shape ascension into the depth of eternity until a suitable time for their re-emergence arrived. If Johann Carl Friedrich Gauss, the German mathematician (d. 1855), who conquered the world of mathematics through his use of brilliant conceptions and aspects and gave a new look to human science and knowledge, was not given patronage by the Duke of Brunswick in his early years and, therefore, freed from the troubles and worries of earning his living, he could not possibly have discovered and introduced those 146 facts into mathematics.[16]

---

[16] Gauss kept a diary of his many discoveries. See *The Shaping of Arithmetic*

If we take a look at the history of nations, we will see that the expressions and announcements of science have most likely been made by the richer countries; though it is not accurate to believe that there have never been people with scientific and advanced minds capable of leading human knowledge among underdeveloped or poorer countries.

Unfortunately, there are more charlatans found in every society than true scholars. Scholars are usually very few and in the minority, and when, because of their conscience and humanitarianism, they introduce their findings to the public, they face the wrath of superstitious people and the accusation of prejudice from demagogues who see their own interests in jeopardy [or such discoveries may be used to harm rather than to heal by the political leaders of times]. In a society like this, a scholar will never find a chance to express him or herself or to discuss his or her findings and discoveries. It has been seen many times that scientific facts and rules are often buried in the pages of books and in the corners of libraries and because of customs, habits and public opinion, they never find a ground for expression. This is why many scholars remain unappreciated, and their works are expressed and issued only after their death by their followers. If there had been any thinker or scholar who, by his or her very sacrifices, opened up the doors and announced the truths for his or her society, he or she would surely have faced Socrates' destiny or the demagogic clerical accusations made against Galileo Galilei.

There are many who criticized scientists for not introducing and describing their discoveries to the public in spite of the absence of favorable conditions. However, as history has shown, ordinary people might judge scientific findings by their very incomplete thoughts and ideas, deny those discoveries, and hence make the scientist's life difficult. It is awkward, however, to think of a scientist as a merchant who must advertise his or her goods, despite unfavorable social and living conditions and the aimless envy of society.

It does not matter how long we remain irrational, the scientist will continue his or her research and fortunate scientific life so that eventually non-essential requests and expectations will vanish. There

after C.F. Gauss's Disquisitiones Arithmeticae, ed. Catherine Goldstein, Norbert Schappacher and Joachim Schwermer (New York: Springer, 2007).

have been, for example, many unfair social effects on the life of Franz Mesmer (German physician, d. 1815), who introduced animal magnetism. Mesmer was made to leave his hometown. He had to earn his living as a physician and continue his research in magnetism and Mesmeristic curing during his spare time. When invited to the Academy of Berlin, he expressed that he felt old and tired from challenging and fighting, and wanted to spend the rest of his life isolated from people.[17]

There is no evidence in the history of humanity to indicate that an honest scientist, a thinker, or an inventor, has entered a scientific field for fame or commercial reasons. Scientists and thinkers continue with their research not necessarily to earn a living and make a profit; otherwise they are but intelligent traders. The intention of an honest inventor is, most likely, stepping towards the advancement of civilization. Movement toward social and human civilization would be stronger, and truth and spirituality in the world would appear more beautiful, if instant profits were not in the mind of humans, and if charlatans—who often mislead the masses—did not usurp the place of the honest thinkers. But, unfortunately, genius always suffers from ignorance and this is its greatest deprivation. It will be a great pity if society does not understand the gentle and sensitive minds of its thinkers and will not encourage them properly.

Several examples in history indicate that there have been numerous misfortunes in the lives of scientists and learned human beings. For example, Augustin-Louis Cauchy (d. 1857), the French mathematician who invented Group Theory, suffered many disasters in his short life, yet because he respected his moral and conscientious duty, he wrote a summary of his vast research in two pages at the time he was dying. Perhaps, he did not want to deprive humanity of his knowledge. But do the deprivations and misfortunes of his life awaken the mind of the uncaring masses?

The integrity of a nation depends on the scientific, scholarly and moral characteristics of its people. Knowledge does not repeat and describe the beliefs and ideas of the past and present. However deep the

---

[17] For more on the theories and work of Franz Mesmer, see *Brain, Mind and Medicine: Essays in Eighteenth-Century Neuroscience*, ed. C.U.M. Smith, Harry Whitaker and Stanley Finger (New York: Springer, 2007) 303.

research and studies into past events may be, it still is an introduction to a new way of life that discovers the hidden mysteries behind science and organizes a civilized plan for the future. There are enormous talents in human society all over the world, and this cannot be denied. In backward societies, universities are often closed to those geniuses who might discover new facts in science, or to artisans who often solve mechanical and physical problems through their work.

A university that does not accept and develop new ideas, as well as positive thoughts, is nothing but a public library in which people review the ideas of the past, which, of course, is wasting time. I do not want to be idealistic; but even if we believe that the use of science is primarily economic, products from a scientific organization, even in its very primary and introductory state, will be no less important than agricultural and mining products. If economic progress and movement are based on the ideas and doctrines of the scientific mind, it will surely work in a more orderly fashion and result in better social economics.

If a human being cannot advance a society and or contribute to its progress, then his or her impact is limited; and the same logic applies to the university. Since a university works like the intellect of the society, it must be at the center to bring up new ideas and develop scientific doctrines, should not limit itself with its economical advantages, but on the expansion of knowledge and scholarship; otherwise, it is like an empty skull and nonfunctioning brain. But if a university cares for and supports new scientific thoughts, thinkers will leave their thoughts and ideas within its hands willingly.

I, like many others, have met talented people in my society who have been eager to study the latest discoveries, to research and find new facts and doctrines and to avoid repetition in their own research. However, though I wished to help them, I could not lead them anywhere unless educational institutes embraced them, open their doors, and welcome talented individuals to their communities.

If a university publishes the latest discoveries and research and leaves these within the reach of people, it will not only help talented individuals but also lead society to many scientific and educational goals. It is also an assurance to the scholar that he will reach his ultimate goal. The issuing of scientific thoughts to the world is a primary and first step toward civilization.

The goals of a living human being are concentrated on any successful way to develop humanity, and if the light of life shines in any society, sooner or later, personal motivations will fade and the reality of civilization will be glorified. The intelligent, learned human being is able to solve difficult problems in life and smooth out the roads toward advanced civilizations for his or her fellow human beings and future generations.

If we do not improve and correct our inner and outer qualities, the presentation of our past, at any given time, will be frightening, disturbing and shameful.

Physicists may show the simple wave by throwing an object into the water and by those circles that appear and develop around the object, from its center to the side of the container. The best description of waves is that they are the result of transmissions.

If we hold a polarized glass and look at the sun carefully, we will see big and small circles that extend from the center of the sun with motions. They are just like waves that appear on the surface of the water. These waves are composed of positive and negative oscillations that appear in clockwise and counterclockwise motions (Sine and Cosine curves). Such oscillations exist on every level of nature, and they are the general expression of natural structures which philosophers, like Democritus (Greek philosopher, d. 370 BC), labeled as undividable portions or atoms.[18]

From the organization of the smallest particle such as an atom, molecule, electron, proton, photon, or other newborn collision of particles (which scientists in our time believe have doubled and improved in quality, and appear as waves and particles), to the gigantic planets and galaxies whose movements and characteristics, the comparisons and relativities of which have made the celestial organized systems, are all the presentation of endless, eternal expanded waves of nature which form beings by expansion and accumulated vibration. The double qualities of the elementary system in nature, as mentioned before as wave and particle, allow one to believe in the continuity and unity of nature as well as metaphysical energies. This does not mean that existence is only material and hence to deny its intrinsic and metaphysical energies or

---

[18] See *The Atomists Leucippus and Democritus*, trans. C.C.W. Taylor (Toronto: University of Toronto Press, 1999). Also see Sylvia Berryman, "Democritus," *The Stanford Encyclopedia of Philosophy* (Winter 2016 Edition), Edward N. Zalta (ed.), URL = <https://plato.stanford.edu/archives/win2016/entries/democritus/>.

even to believe in the material as a figure whose purer energies, which in their extreme are out of our sensory reach to study, lose their shapes and dimensions in the infinite. They appear corporeal and natural because of a range of connected and proportional causes at the time, but, of course, they are not disconnected with the infinite.

Hermann von Helmholtz (German physicist, d. 1894) identifies that at the end one will get to a point when the essential subject of the science of physics is to relate the appearances of nature to those unchangeable attracting and repelling energies, on which their intensity depends for their (interval) distance apart.[19] To understand nature, one must solve this problem. As soon as we relate these natural appearances completely to the simple energies and make sure that this system of energies results in these appearances, science has done its job. If an idea more complete than that of Helmholtz is proven, we can be sure that science has taken its first investigative step toward a true reality that has been proven only through verbal reasoning. Now it will give more accurate reasons to the scholars of different schools of philosophy to prove the truth and the fact of existence. Nevertheless, the ranges of waves, which we have talked about, have temporary forms (molds) that after constant proportional actions and reactions change their place from one figure to another.

If it is possible for a viewer to stand on the point of a wave with natural motion and look at the length of his or her past and future life in the wave which he or she has left or must take, he or she will see all the states, qualities, happenings, and events which were caused by his or her unconscious or conscious mind from the very beginning (as much as vision permits) to the point where he or she now stands. This individual will then be able to study the history of this vital and natural wave as the reality of his or her unfinished book, on the tablet of existence.

This explanation is not unreal because the human spirit, the consciousness and the essence of one's reality, which physicists may refer to it as the fourth dimension, is inclusive of and envelops time and space. All stages, forms, figures, and corporeal limitations are made visible

---

[19] See *Hermann von Helmholtz and the Foundations of Nineteenth-Century Science*, ed. David Cahan (Berkeley: University of California Press, 1993) 474–494.

and observable at the present time. For example, imagine that an ant is traveling from point A to point B in ten minutes, the ant itself which is passing according to the unit of its step, is taking ten minutes to go from A to B, while an observer like us sees the whole distance almost in no time. The story of our body and spirit [force of life] is comparable to this example. Extra-sensory perceptions, predictions, true perceptions, and cognitions show that the spirit or soul is a viewer and dominates over the natural time and space locality of the body and does not obey or follow the time and space to which a body is bonded because of its condition and corporeal limitation. Body is the lower stage of soul: the soul is like a human being and the body is like his or her shadow.

The history of an individual's life, or any living being, is like an infinite film roll on which all events and happenings are recorded. If we want to show this infinite roll in detail, like a motion picture, all the natural happenings of life will appear on the screen. This essential pre-destined which in fact is the absolute free will of the existence, is the essence of the reality of the cosmos, and it leads us to this truth that: the infinite existence is nothing but an absolute action.

Our everyday adventures of life, events, and incidents are not vain and dissolute and will not end in some meaningless myth; but they, too, are recorded with the suitable, detailed presentations on the pages of the past and future, visible to the eye of absolute intellect. If we agree that the presence of a being includes his or her past history, then we do not need to separate the origin of this being from its present presence, but to agree that the core and fact that this being's past that is effective at the present is also a continuous and visible reflection on the page of the infinite. If we consider the system of how a television set or camera works, and understand the transferring of the wave-lights images from one station to another, we notice that a motion that is traveling from one station will return to the same station. It travels through ascending and descending curves, visible to a station that is connected to the original starting point. The law of returning to the origin is acceptable in all of the manifestations originated from a core, a center.

So, we arrive at this point that all beings are predestined, and traces of their essence are marked on the roads of their life. It is on this road onto which their footprints have extended figures and forms are reviewable for the rational individual. At each level of existence, each road appears to inherit the realities and positions of its past. Action and reaction are but two impressions of the same act. For example, if in a suitable season of the year a plant faces a disaster because a gardener forgets to water it on the third month of spring, the effect of this neglect will appear gradually in the yellow faded leaves of the plant after two months. Then no compensation will be useful to amend the damages of the past. I think this understanding needs to open up a new chapter in medical science, because it helps us understand the ways to heal an illness sooner and better if we look for and into the causes in past history. Psychological research done shows that inheritance and environmental inputs shape an individual so that these factors have a direct influence on his present well-being.

One thing is certain, natural existence is traveling from an eternal unknown point (unknown to human being) to another eternal unknown point, a journey from itself to itself, with no delays, stops, or investigations. Human being, too, is marking his or her impressions and effects along this mysterious path. An individual's deeds, thoughts, acts, and imagination are acquiring form and shape, apparently and inwardly in infinite nature, while his present being is the center of his past and an introduction to the direction of his future journey. A human being's physical and spiritual life, harmonious with the passing of time, is reflected onto the face of existence, and our present fate, as mentioned before, is an unfinished book including those events that appear as heavy compositions on the screen of life. None of our past physical and mental happenings will be eliminated and forgotten, because the book of creation has them stable and fixed upon its pages, our own history will manifest itself as soon as the conditions are suitable. At that time, we will find that all the events are alive, present and real, and they exist and stand with all their conditions. Our being will be an index and the consequence of those happenings, legends and stories.

Every sound expressed, every word uttered has its own characteristics and remains on a special wave line. Each journeys to the utmost extent of the universe keeping its qualities and wavelength presentable to and receivable by a receptive and suitable receiver. This is very similar to those black and white reflections of a film appearing on the space between the origin and screen. It seems as if pictures have natural form only in their origin and destination [screen], whereas those reflected qualities, compositions and pictures are also present in the space between the origin and the screen. But changes in the expansion and accumulation of black and white, shadows and lights, which appear differently in the film roll and the screen, are misleading and cause one not to recognize that they are the presentations of the same things. If we take a closer look, we will see that those are but particles, atoms, molecules, waves, and metaphysical energies that make up those figures. This eternal presentation, which appears differently in different stages of existence, is the appearance of that natural reality visible for a human being when it coincides with his or her sense and is recognizable more through his or her energies. We recognize the events when they are in harmony with our senses perception and faculties of mind; we recognize the core of those events when we access our inner energy and abstract intellect.

This is, of course, a natural principle based on physical impressions; every thing on every level of existence follows this law according to a predestined order set by an absolute free will of the Absolute. At the present time, we have the impressions of those past qualities handed to us through a special time wave. These imprints present themselves in the wrinkles of our brains, the book of our memory, and in the magnetic waves of our corporal body. And, at the present time, when we try to stabilize and focus on our present journey, the past becomes forgotten, and the future remains unknown to us.

The moral traditions and decent leaders, as well as the learned individuals whose conscience eye is open to observe the reality, have always encouraged their people to regard praiseworthy and worthy deeds, thoughts and purposes, they have encouraged their community to take steps towards peace and honoring humanity. They have warned the selfish of an eternal death. These great individuals taught this invisible and important truth by their own example.

The character of the knowledgeable and wise individuals is dissolved into the very essence of the absolute; the absolute that leads their thoughts and their deeds. Such inner discovery presents itself in their words of wisdom, in their actions and in their teachings. To follow their wisdom and their teachings is like seeing through a powerful lens that helps us to distinguish between prosperity and adversity, between morality and cruelty, between praiseworthy and wickedness.

Particles are like numbers, apparently limited but in reality unlimited. Nothing in the universe contrasts with the factual principles, systems, and the wisdom of the universe. Details, in the limited surroundings do not hold generality; but at their very core they are infinite and thus universal.

If we take a look at temporal and hypothetical physical laws, we will see that the units of the human body are different and sometimes in constant disagreement with the human being's conscious perceptions and understanding. Contrast and opposition are made by imaginary limitations and relative comparisons between incidents. Good and bad, eternal and transient, light and darkness, motion and stillness, existence and non-existence, and many others are the outcomes of our imaginative comparisons. They are the products of the limited and unreal observations of our senses; senses that are restricted in their limitations and bound by their own circumstances. Absolute reality, therefore, is not recognized until these limitations are broken and or dissolved.

We know about the uncertainty of views gathered by the senses. If we use the laws of the Earth's gravity or electromagnetic wave energies coming from millions of galaxies, of suns which make axes of living circulations for inhabitants of the planets; and, when we use wave expansion or accumulation as the unit of our perceptions, we only arrive at some approximate opinion; such opinions or figurative facts will not lead a seeker or a researcher to understand the mysteries of existence. The mysteries of existence are only understood in infinity where their limitations are broken, and they are free from dimensions. But as soon as the conceptions of the mind and imagination gather a picture from the sense perception carrier, the principles of time, space, mass measurement, motion, and other dimensional influences and qualities will surround the conscious mind. They are like a silkworm cocoon! They cloud the intellect by their superficial appearance and unreal halos; thus will not allow the individual to recognize the core of a notion and perceive and analyze it by an abstract logic beyond the ordinary. It is obvious that limitations are perceived by our senses, and limitations can only be understood in the dimensions of measurement, time, space, etc.; thus will not open a door towards understanding outside of these limitations. For example, the outstanding principles understood by Newton and Kepler, weaken when we have learned about a comet that traveled about 550 kilometers per second and was 52,000 kilometers from the Sun. These exceptional events, events beyond our control, will transform our understanding of our present laws, and the reality and the laws of the eternal remain beyond the grasp of our limitations.

The gravitational weight of a body, which has a definite weight on Earth, is two and a half times heavier on Jupiter and is lighter on Venus and lighter still on Orus, a planet fifty kilometers in diameter.[20] These differences make us notice the relativities. Within the limitations of a galaxy, if time is considered a fourth dimension, then like any other new but imaginary principle, it is also considered original; but, when we witness other manifestations, rising from the very core of the existence, then the sweetness of those old philosophies disappears, and the laws introduced by the temporal comparisons will be considered as obsolete.

This fourth dimension, as a nonessential matter, will appear irrational and loses its nobility automatically like any other dream as we advance. Cause and effect, motion and stillness, potentiality and actuality, are all like the above principle. Sense and perception have to fall within our human-made logic, for every change and transition we need to rely on a dimensional reason. We create logical reasoning for every contradiction and unfounded matter in order to make them believable to ourselves! Particles and elements do not obey our made up laws when studied independently. As soon as they are placed in "relationship" with other elements and particles, we give them names and definitions so we recognize them! These names and definitions are not real. If a square, a triangle or circulating and straight motion is examined by general standards, we arrive at the principle of regularity, but does the escaped electron or gases follow and adopt our laws? For example, every second of the 24-hour rotation of the Earth, which has a special position in the cosmos, possesses an incomparable appearance and every minute of

---

[20] There is a specific relationship between gravity, mass and distance; see Ron Hipschman, "Your Weight on Other Worlds," *Exploratorium*, URL = <https://www.exploratorium.edu/ronh/weight/>.

this rotation specifically defines its orbit, which is the outcome of the principle of regularity. Gases move in a disorderly direction, and they represent partial, physical manifestation (this is the last and unfinished observation). In the irregularity of their movements they still obey the general discipline and order of the universe. In order to make it clear, let us take an example. Suppose we want to make a ball from 50 meters of rope. When we start to roll the rope our fingers and the rope constantly cross. To make a complete, spherical bulk, the point of intersection has to cross an irregular direction around the hypothetical surface of the ball; otherwise, if the point regularly crossed a repeated direction, it would not make that complete spherical ball.

Therefore, if one wants to make a law for the motion of a being's moving point, one has to rely on irregular motions, like that of gases. If this fact were not reliable, the motion of those mobile points and the agent that rolls the rope would not give us a regular and orderly result. This explanation prompts one to recall Sir James Jeans (English physicist and mathematician, d. 1946) who talks about the catastrophic or tidal theory, and writes about The Dynamical Theory of Gases (1904).[21]

Since we, bound to our limitations, cannot completely follow in the present condition the direction of an irregular particle from its beginning to infinity, therefore, we may exclude irregular motions and portions represented by certain factors from the general law of regularity. This prompts one to believe in regularity as a general, universal law and to rely on it since one has not seen in usual, orbital motions anything but regularity. If creation had a beginning and a starting point, and one could observe and follow all the primary motions of every natural detail (where atom organization is counted), the irregularity of gases could be generalized. This idea makes one almost positive that even these irregular forms, or the wandering planets, are making regular organizations. If appearances and effects are visible to a scientific eye, then the comprehension of truth should become more readily apparent.

When I look at a flower beatified by its fragrance and freshness I ask myself from where does all its elegance, grace and order come from? How do its branches, leaves and interlaced roots cross everywhere

---

[21] For information see James Jeans, *The Dynamical Theory of Gases* (Cambridge: Cambridge University Press, 1925).

through the masses of mud to find living energy of life? They carefully search and extract every portion and particle of the soil in order to find purity and tenderness. This reminds me of the skillful artists who mix colors on their painting board and carefully use their susceptible eyes with constant precision. They overlook their surroundings but are focused on one place, the canvas. They brush slowly and precisely to create and give life to the delicateness of their artistic mind, with such mathematical precision; they let the potential of their thoughts reflect on the canvas; and undo their possible mistakes. But the destiny of the flower and its life, drawn by the powerful brush of nature, will never stop nor will it make a mistake. It works on its art slowly and precisely until a beautiful flower appears. One can always ask in which part of that harsh, wooden branch or dark interlaced roots was this colorful, delicate, elegant, and fragrant flower hidden? How did it bloom? Or if magnetic and atmospheric rays and waves help this plant to grow, where was this duty appointed and who arranged for it? Why does it still follow its movement in such a hurry and search every portion of the atmosphere to reach its spiritual and or mystical destination? What is it looking for, stretching to the sky? The smell of its fragrance spreads all over the space, extents almost everywhere. It acts like a newcomer who gracefully flatters and makes everyone appreciate its beauty and grace. It desires to expand, to dissolve into infinity, to journey to eternity. From where does this eagerness for eternity and infinity come? And where is that mysterious and secret core that leads this flower to its destiny; the essence that human mind cannot recognize or perceive? One thing is certain: Nature's wisdom and intellect has a long, unmistaken will; and the living destiny of her people and elements are apparent in her actions, reactions and influence. It is strange that all living animals, plants, objects, and human beings are like evaporated water under the influence and effect of this authority—they love and are attracted by their eternal destiny and walk to the heavens of their inherent being. Where does the Earth search in its day and night and why is it wandering and restless, traveling so hastily to unknown points, even unknown to itself?

Who is this Attractor and where is Its location; the Absolute that attracts, draws all the galaxies, planets, stars, moons, human beings, animals, plants, and objects to their destiny? The whole existence is attracted to such a powerful, and eternal command according to its own potentiality and aptitude. The most Exalted that draws the Being into this endless attraction; where is this most Glorified if not everywhere, how does It command, if not from the depth of the Essence, from the depth of the heart of everything that exists. The one who is free from the thoughts of others, is the one who discovers and understands the reality of existence. As Spinoza (Dutch philosopher, d. 1677) so beautifully distinguishes, the intellect and body are not substantially different, but merely two dreams of God's manifestations which have appeared in two separate ways. "Whatever is, is in God, and nothing can be or be conceived without God" [22] because God is both body and soul, and, in fact, there is no essence but God.

---

[22] For more information and a summary overview of many of his works, see Steven Nadler, "Baruch Spinoza," *The Stanford Encyclopedia of Philosophy* (Summer 2020 Edition), Edward N. Zalta (ed.), URL = <https://plato.stanford.edu/archives/sum2020/entries/spinoza/>.

The more the eye of the heart sees and becomes conscious the more a human being is able to admit to his limitation before the knowledge of the existence; and this is the first step that any knowledgeable human being should take towards understanding.

The most learned human being is one whose character is in harmony with the essence of nature, even though his or her identity with nature may appear as something mystical.

There is nothing for which a human being cannot find a complete example of it in his or her own being. One of the reasons that we may not realize our own eminent position in the universe of being is our sense distraction, and sense distraction is nothing but the limitation and boundaries of sense perceptions. If a human being purifies his own self (*nafs*) from whatever is not the reality of the self, he will understand the importance of his own being, he will learn his name in the design of being, his magnificence that is the presentation of the Real in the world of multiplicity. He is the reality of the "great name" (*ism-i a'zam*), his humanity, his representation of the sacred that is hidden behind the veils of nature.

Abul-Abass Amuli (Persian mystic, 11th century), one of the great Sufis of his time, was asked to perform a miracle. He replied, "What miracle is greater and more important than my own life? I was a business man spending my days with business; but once the Divine light illuminated my heart, great mystics like Kharaqani (Persian Sufi master, 11th century) and Abul-Khayr (Persian Sufi master, 11th century) come to visit me and ask my teachings." The virtue that Abul-Abass Amuli is talking about is not gathered through adapted knowledge and information, but the illumination of heart. When he stops relying on the appearances and confinements, his inner eye (heart) opens to understand the depths of the sacred Absolute. His virtue came from meaning not through forms and figures. He eliminated the superfluous from his being until he arrived at the point of unification seeing the Sacred Absolute wherever he looked.

The way of a learned individual is simple yet impossible. The sensibility of intelligent minds and sense perception may lead us to see and perceive everything keenly and deeply, and remember details. Yet we have to go a little further than observing and remembering, we are to search for fact behind external observation, we are to look for the essence of things. Nature has given these qualities to everyone of us; yet it is the wise person who searches and finds.

We have heard many things about leaders of humanity, especially moral leaders. For example, although great leaders have displayed sympathy and gentleness when facing even a small injustice, they have shown great bravery, strength of adjudication and justice as well. This is true balance for a complete and complementary being who remains in the balance between manifestations and reality. These are the delicate qualities of moral and wise leaders that become the heroes of humanity.

I have seen individuals who present themselves as educators and spent time carelessly attempting to discover the ways of wisdom presented by moral and wise teachers. Sometimes they may even look at the mind-process of a scientist, an educator, and an inventor to explain how a scientist invented or explained a physical or metaphysical problem. In their thoughtless way of investigation they have always followed a very long, imaginary, unrealistic path that has not only led them away from useful results but also caused them to lose their objective. They waste days and even years explaining something that may not be useful or open any door towards understanding after all. And when they get tired, they become hopeless and see their attempts as useless. They often interrupt and disregard their thoughts; and they will even spend hours and days explaining and discussing their useless, imaginary direction and common, unrealistic imagination, with no intention of proving anything.

I remember once I was invited to an educational and cultural meeting many years ago. The host was a friend of mine and the program included a presentation and a lecture. The invited lecturer could not attend the meeting that night. The host, who knew me quite well, asked me to take over the lecture and talk about the appointed subject. Selfishness, which I called friendship and cooperation that day, made me accept the request. The host was very pleased and left me with much thanks.

At the meeting I gave an unprepared speech about a subject, and although I don't remember the relationship between those monumental matters and the points which my mind was quickly gathering and assuredly explaining behind that podium (which surely was not based on any minutely thoughtful or scientific origination), my speaking influenced the audience in such a way that it made me believe I had solved and discussed some unsolved problems and mysteries. The truth was that the audience habitually appreciated and encouraged any energetic lecturer, and because my lecture was a composite of past and present ideas about science, psychology and literature it was a diversion from the meeting. I did not explain the ideas of great individuals as they were written and composed in books, but I offered the indifferent audience some incomplete ideas, one after the other; my intention was to fill time and free my friend from anxiety, worry and shame, and, of course, make the audience aware of my knowledge and eloquence if it were possible.

I have often noticed the same interesting story in many speeches, even those that were given by famous speakers. For example, in one very special ceremony a speaker talked about one of his travels in the world but it was not clear why he was so hopeful and happy about what he had done. Was it the subject which had astonished and occupied his mind and thought, or was it the silent, astonished, staring, and even disinterested looks of the audience which permitted this individual to talk about any insignificant subject he wished so freely?

Knowledgeable individuals and scientists always try to avoid talking nonsense. When they speak, they are usually certain that their words are based on some principles and facts and also that their audience is competent. I don't mean to criticize the speaker who attends gatherings and meetings. It is obvious that an orator who gives a lecture to a group of people respects words, and spends time in the preparation of his or her talk. At the same time, it is not fair if we believe that an audience is always un-informed or uninterested.

I think that the introduction made by a speaker behind the podium, and the shaking heads of the audience—which they keep moving like the pendulum of a clock until time is up—help to confirm anything which the speaker says. These are the signs of selfishness that are present in both the speaker's and listeners' behavior. Although these scenes have never been criticized or avoided, they do not own any scientific approval. Repeating and studying moral values to show people their individual and social duties is worthwhile, and explaining scientific ideas and discoveries to enlighten people should never be underestimated, but common and dull speeches in meetings and between people, or even in personal and individual investigation, is trite and vain. They may be good conversational interactions but do not open any door to knowledge and understanding.

Friedrich Hegel (German philosopher, d. 1831) identifies that there are both truths and mistakes, rights and wrongs, between people and their thoughts, but searching for and discussing truth is the job for a great individual.[23] A person who can discover, explain and teach the thing that is needed in his decade is the great individual of his or her time.

If a human being is known to be knowledgeable merely because he or she pronounces some eloquent, rhymed words, with no use for people, then he or she is selfish. Long ago I met a man who was famous and known as a scholar and I really was very astonished and surprised when, as soon as he met me, even though he was not sure if I was even interested in his words or not, he began to talk and explain things because he wished to hear himself talk. The purpose was not to make me understand ideas but to make me confess to the vastness of his knowledge.

We read in Saint Augustine's (theologian and philosopher, d. 430 AD) writings that truths remain hidden from human's eyes because human often becomes the victim of what he has to conquer.[24] In his famous trial, Socrates in his own defense talked about the oracle of Delphi and asked Apollo if there was anyone more learned and wiser than Socrates. After a while he heard a voice say that there was no one wiser than Socrates. When Socrates heard the story he thought that he was not very knowledgeable, but he was certain that God would not

---

[23] See Georg Wilhelm Friedrich Hegel, *The Philosophy of History* (New York: Dover, 1956). Also see Georg Wilhelm Friedrich Hegel, *The Phenomenology of the Spirit*, trans. Terry Pinkard (New York: Cambridge University Press, 2018). For an overview of Hegel's thought, see Redding, Paul, "Georg Wilhelm Friedrich Hegel," *The Stanford Encyclopedia of Philosophy* (Winter 2020 Edition), Edward N. Zalta (ed.), URL = <https://plato.stanford.edu/archives/win2020/entries/hegel/>.

[24] See *The Confessions of St. Augustine*, trans. John K. Ryan (New York: Random House, 1960).

tell a lie. It took him a long time to think about this matter. He came to the conclusion that perhaps because he (Socrates) knew that he did not know, perhaps the voice meant that the wisest among human being is the one who confesses his ignorance, as Socrates did.[25]

My teacher, Mir Ghotbeddin (Persian mystic, d. 1962), always taught that virtue was in the listening ears and not in the speaking tongue. A wise teacher is a keen and true student of absolute beauty and truth, and searches everywhere for them with all his or her heart. A human being can harmonize with truth instead of praising himself or herself. He or she can work like a powerful crane able to move the great weight by using little energy.

Herbert Spencer (English philosopher, d. 1903) suggests that learning the meaning of things is more useful than learning the meaning of words and terms, whether for mental, ethical, physical, or educational reasons. He also contends that scrutinizing happenings is more important than acquiring the use of language and words in a culture.[26]

The acquaintance and harmony of wisdom with truth in nature brings knowledge. When the function of senses becomes something more than touching and being in apparent harmony with the figures and forms of things, then the human intellect and wisdom acquire an intellectual and qualitative insight with every observation. It is at this point that a human being's sense observation and perceptional limitations change in accord with reality. At that time, the intrinsic knowledge of the soul and wisdom remains in harmony with the knowledge of the nature. This is the place when a human being confesses his or her ignorance [his or her limited knowledge] and begins to realize the extensiveness of the knowledge of the existence and thus will search to understand the eternity and the infinity of the Being from within.

Immanuel Kant (German philosopher, d. 1804) says that beauty, or any beautiful thing, will not reveal the outside world to us, but it shows and indicates our own special state of soul.[27] Benefits of things

---

[25] See Plato, *The Last Days of Socrates*, trans. Christopher Rowe (New York: Penguin, 2010).

[26] See *The Philosophy of Herbert Spencer*, trans. Michael W. Taylor (New York: Continuum, 2007).

[27] See Immanuel Kant, *Observations on the Feeling of the Beautiful and Sublime*, trans. John T. Goldthwait (Berkeley: University of California Press, 1960).

do not beautify them; since those qualities are hidden from and unclear to us. There is a strength and energy in them that excite our intellect, and relate to our wisdom and sense of morality. They harmonize their benefits with our perceptions. We do not perceive the tunes of things, rather what we perceive is our own potentials.

Death is an evolutional and developmental ladder of beings that veils the Absolute, the veils that are torn away. Death and life are two reciprocal appearances presenting themselves as the stages of existence. Otherwise, existence is an Absolute whole that includes the stages of being.

Birth and death are images of change. They follow a predestined evolution and reach that freedom for which conditions have already been prepared in the universe. Physical and metaphysical scientists tell us that those grounds of change extend from physiology and anatomy to psychology and ethics. The solitary, abstract soul (*ruh-i mujarad*) stimulates the proponents of evolution in a world of possibilities. It wears different suits, presents itself in different forms, harmonious with the condition of its being. Before entering this corporal life, it ascended through various stages of ability and capability one after the other. According to the same principle, it followed and accepted the forms and facilities of the physical presence to organize and continue its present natural life. Therefore, after death it had to neutralize its previous attempts and obtain other suitable equipment to become harmonious with its environment and surrounding. It followed these stages until it reached an absolute freedom, and, as Descartes said, every change in the world had a place in the general principle.[28]

In one of his books on the principles of nature, Leibniz indicates that birth develops naturally and gradually; it gives a human being a chance to study and investigate it.[29] But death turns everything back very quickly. It happens suddenly and severely, which makes every

[28] See Desmond Clarke, *Descartes' Philosophy of Science* (Manchester: Manchester University Press, 1982) 92. Also see René Descartes, *Principles of Philosophy*, trans. Valentine Rodger Miller and Reese P. Miller (Netherlands: Springer, 2012); René Descartes, *Discourse on Method and Related Writings*, trans. Desmond Clarke (New York: Penguin, 1993).

[29] See Benson Mates, *The Philosophy of Leibniz* (Oxford: Oxford University Press, 1986) 42; Nicholas Rescher, *On Leibniz* (Pittsburgh: University of Pittsburgh Press, 2013) 376. Also see Nicholas Jolley, *Leibniz* (New York: Routledge, 2006).

investigation and observation very difficult. If there were any intensity in the changes from life to death, births, deaths and lifetime races and remains of fossils, old primitive animals, cylindrical bacteria and primitive algae, which are found nowadays, would be understood.

The beginnings of green algae multiplication and the self-multiplication of some bacteria are the kind of puzzles that have been investigated as the traces of existence traverse through nature. But, so far, there has not been a satisfactory solution. The principle of completion is set so perfectly and leads nature on its journey; this principle is so perfect that understanding and witnessing its every angle seems to be an impossible task. Although the precise eye of the investigator cannot possibly see every angle of this gradual change, it is astounded by whatever it does see. Since these changes come gradually, they make the measuring of changes in natural bodies possibly but difficult. This is something that cannot be denied: existence is always held in a precarious balance between life and death. This principle has introduced the table of existence. A clear example of this natural current is the once-a-year molting of the snake. These changes are not measurable precisely. Giving a different example, suppose we put a bowl full of water on the fire. As soon as heat begins to warm the water, the temperature of the water rises until it boils. This takes place gradually, but to the viewer the boiling of the water has happened in a short time; and will disappear at once to nowhere, although it seems that an event may appear or disappear at a specific time, or all of a sudden, with no forewarning, but we must know that the process is always gradual.

Waiting for things to happen, disregarding every possibility and every step no matter how small, is like disconnecting the unity of a cause from its effect. The truth is that there is no cause without effect, and no event is possible without an overall, visible and essential condition; though cause and effect seem to have no continuity in location or time. Anyway, the stages and transitions foster the newborns of possibilities.

The Absolute soul (*ruh-i mujarad*), or the essence of life, has been studied for centuries by many scientists and learned individuals. The Absolute is free from any decoration and impurities, and, it is the identity that presents a human being at the present time. It appears from behind colorful glasses and in different wraps. Sometimes it manifests itself as natural science and knowledge, and on other occasions it appears under the wraps of corruption and deviation. It is, however, free from all these causes and relationships, since it is an eternal principle, an Absolute. We heard that whatever comes from the soil will go back to it, and whatever comes from the heavens will return to its origin. Absolute knowledge is free from all these limitations and colorful decorations. And since the manifestations are not the causes of its existence, then manifestations will not cause it to disappear either.

The wisdom that has journeyed with me throughout my existence, and in the stages of Being, will remain with me to my second birth, and the second birth is not my demise. If we look deeply and clearly into our motives, good or bad, and distinguish them from the truth of our identity, then we will understand the quality of the after death.

Isthmuses, and passages, have a common boundary with each other. According to the law of natural existence, although they seem, at intervals, to reach different levels, they don't have distinct and independent boundaries from each other. Like Newton's spectrum of lights, they have different specifications: red is differentiated from green and, therefore, have different wavelengths.[30] All of these wavelengths have been measured from 1/1000 angstrom to 3000 microns. But in a natural reflection observed from the prism, there is no defined boundary to separate any of these colors. Red gradually becomes orange, light yellow, amber, yellowish green, green blue, violet and ultra violet. This is an approximate representation of the spectrum. There is not any specified boundary between these colors in the reflection chart. Isthmuses and intervals also make life contrast with death, even though death and life are born from each other and do not have a distinct boundary from each other. The unity and sameness that prevails in every material, or spiritual, stage makes the philosophy of materialism doubtful. The absolute rule of matter over nature, especially in the revolution of human existence, is not without objection.

The ideas of materialistic philosophers are usually based on a hypothesis drawn from the natural change of sense and a deduction based on sensual conceptions. Materialists have not and will not recognize the principles of existential originality through current and

---

[30] See Isaac Newton, *Opticks: Or A Treatise of the Reflections, Refractions, Inflections, and Colours of Light*, 4th ed. Gale ECCO, Print Editions, 2018.

assimilated natural changes. In fact, the correct way of investigating a difficult problem is not just to accept things that are observable while denying things of which our senses have not a complete knowledge. It is not correct to placate our mind with simple logic.

Once I had a discussion with one of my philosopher friends who had materialistic ideas. The discussion of that day may help to posit some reasons for a belief in eternity of the soul, or the essence of life. There is no need to deny the eternity of matter or energy and the noble principle that says that nothing will be lost in this universe.[31] On the other hand, this principle does not limit existence to materialistic combinations and impressions.

My friend insisted on the ideas of materialistic philosophers and wanted to prove that the universe is nothing but a mechanistic, unconscious world in order to present such reasoning. My mind is not opposed to knowledge, and I don't accept any method blindly or deny excellent thoughts out of prejudice. But it is not fair to prefer weak foundations to theories of sound principles. If observations, experiments, experiences, and reasoning do not follow an organized arrangement and correct conditions, they will result in many mistakes and increase our ignorance, not knowledge.

I had to explain the being of a human being from his microscopic stage through the passing of time for my inquisitive friend. I explained that natural and materialistic organizations would eventually be replaced by some other phenomena after changes occurred in their forms and figures. This would be a continual change in their appearance not only before birth and during their lifetime but also after death. Because the cells of the brain and nervous system change very slowly, people think they are everlasting, or at least stable for a lifetime to record and arrange memory. No parts or organs in the body provide a human being with his or her identity [self-hood], because continual change can't result in a stable identity. The reason for our misunderstanding is obvious, since identity is always contiguous with matter and our observations are limited to the sense perceptions. We even believe in our dimensional

---

[31] The First Law of Thermodynamics says that energy can neither be created nor destroyed. See Peter Atkins, *The Laws of Thermodynamics* (Oxford: Oxford University Press, 2010).

experiences as true knowledge, whereas the organs of the body are merely there to obey our identity. There is a hypothesis in physics which says: The inside energy of an isolated body equals zero.[32] Materialistic philosophers have sometimes used this hypothesis to prove their point. They may say that the world is nothing but a composite of mechanical and automatic actions and reactions[33] that acts like a clock!

I have explained in *Chante*[34] that since effect is completely the manifestation and index of cause, therefore, it confirms and proves the existence of the inventor and the invention. In other words, if we analyze and separate the initial thought of the inventor, which is his or her reality, from the instruments of the invention, we have separated the actual principle from the invention and there will remain no invention at all.

Let us continue to consider the clock and its system as our example and suppose that the clock has not been invented yet.

A thinker studies the cosmic movements to compute and understand time. He or she thinks of an instrument to show the time. The first step the thinker takes is to visualize an imaginary vision of the invention in his or her mind. Then the thinker develops the idea and with the help of some tools he or she makes an instrument and our clock begins to work. Here are some points of importance that we should notice: knowledge is more necessary than evidence. If we separate knowledge from evidence, the evidence will make no sense and have no meaning. In other words, if we take the knowledge of the inventor away from his or her invention, there will remain no invention, no clock! Therefore, the clock's existence results from the inventor's knowledge; and any idea or invention must have the traces of its inventor's being.

The actuality is the inventor's intellect. The existence of the inventor and his or her abstract intellect are necessary for every invention. But the apparatus and the instruments of the invention are not essential to the existence of the inventor. If a carpenter, who has the knowledge of

---

[32] The First Law of Thermodynamics shows that in an isolated system, which cannot exchange heat or work with its surroundings, the change in internal energy is equal to zero. For more information see: https://www.toppr.com/guides/physics/thermodynamics/first-law-of-thermodynamics/

[33] See Robin Gordon Brown and James Ladyman, *Materialism: A Historical and Philosophical Inquiry* (New York: Taylor & Francis, 2019).

[34] See Shah Maghsoud's *Chante* (Tehran: Misbahi Publisher, 1962).

carpentry, does not have the equipment to present his or her knowledge, it does not mean that the carpenter doesn't have any knowledge. This and many other examples like this can explain the relationship between human identity and the body. They prove that soul or life energy is not condensed matter, and its existence does not depend on the existence of matter.

My friend, who had a background in materialistic philosophy, had thoughts that resembled those of John Stewart Mill[35] (English philosopher, d. 1873) that, the concept of self and character comes when the mind perceives things and these things remain in memory. Then the mind collects past sensations and estimates their possibilities in the future. By this collecting and comparing the mind imagines a unique matter that is called "I" and believes it to be its self and character. The conception of external materials is also the result of the association of ideas that are collecting and composing sensations, because the mind records and composes whatever is sensible and imagines things and bodies from these sensations.

When analyzing the ideas of these philosophers we arrive at this conclusion: that character change constantly and do not have any stable point of contact during their lifetime. Sense observations and experiences happen repeatedly, and every time they occur they possess special characteristics totally different from what they were before. Since the mind and memory of a human being collect these particulars, his or her character is constantly changing and developing.

Suppose a person loses his memory in an accident, and again he remembers those lost memories in another accident. This person does not show any irregularity in his activity; he merely does not understand things and their uses. But he tries to recognize and understand things and use them properly. His investigation and wish to recognize and understand things is reason to believe in an innate knowledge. Such innate knowledge has an internal motive, and that is an identity [selfhood], and its faculties are not the outcome of the outside world. Now suppose the illness of this person lasts for one year. He continuously collects natural and sense experiences. He, of course, examines these

---

[35] See Elijah Millgram, *John Stuart Mill and the Meaning of Life* (Oxford: Oxford University Press, 2019).

basic experiences like children. He perceives things and decides to carry out or dismiss them with the help of his memory and the association of ideas. But when his cells once again become healthy, his memories come back, and he works like a person who wakes up from sleep. He remembers past experiences and will use those memories that have helped him collect and compare simple feelings. In other words, he forgets and dismisses these memories. This example raises some questions: How are these identities different from his view? Does this forgetful "I" know that essential and old "I"? Does his "I" change over these incidents? Or the memory-incidents change and the "I" remains? The essential identity, which employs and dismisses sense experiences and qualifications, proves that it is a knowledgeable identity that knows the various kinds of experiences. It knows which of its present faculty must be used and how to employ any facility in the body system to calm itself.

None of the body organs and or blood cells are at the dictates of the human will. They don't ask us for help in order to continue their life. They do what is suitable according to the universal order and arrangement of existence. For example, when a germ enters the body, body systems and instruments reject it without knowledge of the human will. It is only after a few days of continuing challenge between the prior germ and its newborn assailants, with the gradual rising of the body's temperature, that one notices illness in his body. It has already been quite a few hours since the blood's white cells began their arranged and thought-out method of attack on the germs in order to send new cells into combat. All of these actions take place and will last until the problem is completely resolved without the interference of the human will. It is obvious that body cells work similarly and no spiritual or ethical qualities can be related to them. These qualities of the lighter bodies are related to the animal soul or human magnetic energies. Animal soul and human magnetic energies are internals between bodies, waves and solitary soul. They rule over their bridges that are the stages of their existence. Their manifestations and appearances on nature are according to their predestined dependence upon nature. Therefore, events and happenings are not the organizers or the factors of the originals (eternal), but originals determine the limitations and boundary of the happenings and teach them their conditions.

Anyway, the changeable particles and waves are not in the position to give birth to an unchangeable stable identity: the "I" of the self. When I look at my own life, I notice many obvious and hidden changes in the natural direction of my body. I see that there have been many things that I did not know, but then I learned. I learned many unnecessary things that I did not use so I forgot them. And even when my mind was blank, without any concepts or experiences, I was still "I". Still I am as I was and, despite all of these changes, I do not see any change in my identity. That was me who insisted on, or dispensed with, something. And it was me who compared the external observation with the subjects. And I created things as much with my mind as was and will be permitted. I have obtained this power and knowledge from an extensive existence. This "I" is not limited and bound to a figure and body; therefore, it cannot be recognized through the limited impressions and aspects of the body, especially from a changeable and unstable figure. So, this "I", who has been noble and stable in two different states, remains stable and noble in all similar states according to the rule of stability.

A while ago I read in one of Swami Vivekanada's (Indian mystic, d. 1902) books that a human consists of a body, a self and a true substance which is the human identity (soul). This identity is hidden behind the body and self. The body is the external cover and the self is the internal cover of the soul. The soul makes everything acquainted with the body. It influences the body with its internal and carnal organs. It is an immortal and non-materialistic essence. It does not follow the principle of cause and effect. It is eternal; therefore, it has no beginning and ending.

My noble identity and stable, innate being has not changed during my lifetime, so that I do not have any reason to believe that it did not exist before birth and will not exist after death. An existence, a being an entity that does not change at different times is noble and immortal.

We read in the narratives of the earliest text about Krishna [Divine Sacred in Hinduism] who says that this world has been created and expanded by his hand, but he is not known to everyone. Everything has found its form through his power and potentiality. They all are in him who was and is eternal. But they are not in his grand substance. Ask yourself what mystery is this that his soul creates everything he chooses, but he himself, is free of everything else.

Extensive everyday expectation of a human being is like veils and walls standing between the individual and the reality. These walls prevent human beings from seeing their fortune and innate worth. They become blind to the core and reality within and so they take falsehood as real.

If desires and wishes, as they were made manifest in the mind, coincided with human destiny, and became real as soon as they were visualized in our imagination, the appearance of the world would change and pain and sadness would seem like penalty. I have seen people review their imaginary wishes as though those unfounded desires were full of joy and pleasure. They have gentle smiles on their face and their cells, muscles and facial nerves perform a dance full of happiness. They act as though they are sleeping and have forgotten their corporeal factual world and common daily life. Unfortunately, desires and wishes have no stable and realistic logic and are not built on firm foundations.

Self-indulgent and made-up desires, which paint unrealistic and colorful pictures on the faces of thought, promote hopelessness, misfortune and coldness in a human being's body and soul. The needy, the one in need of anything, may make up desires and imaginary ideas of magnificent palaces full of good drink, tasty food, costly clothes, and the companionship of important people; he or she imagines being entertained in that aristocratic party. If illogical and unrealistic desires become powerful and begin to control our brains, self and imagination, the first step we take will be onto a dangerous road that ends in misfortune and unhappiness.

The picture of unrealistic dreams and desires is often similar to the painted faces of masked people. They are polished and attractive, but in reality they hide and cover vital cells and nerves; they paint over pain, they are the pictures transforming real individuals into unreal persona. Those who ignorantly smile at these faces, take them as real, and welcome them into their own reality are to needlessly face the misfortunes and miseries hidden in the hearts of those flames.

Desires are endless; we are not satisfied with what we have, no matter what position we are in. We often do not welcome peace into our lives. Desires and unfounded wishes are like quicksand—they are invisible but they consume those who welcome them. No matter how much we pour water into sandy deserts, they remain dry and thirsty. Whose thoughts can saturate these endless sands or survive the quicksand? Only the one who innocently or ignorantly searches for peace in the land of chaos. If a human being is captivated and deceived by his own unrealistic wishes, he will not value the present moment of life but remains anxious about a vague future.

An individual, who daydreams about his attractive yet unknown, fictitious and unrealistic wishes, is like a thirsty individual who imagines water in the middle of a desert. Any time he gets closer to that imaginary water and digs deeper, he finds nothing, yet loses his own self, his own vitality, in the midst of all those mirages. So is the story of our unfounded imagination, and wishful yet unrealistic desires; we will lose our own self, this most worthy gift given to us by the existence, in our illusions; we deprive ourselves from the fruit of self-confidence that moves the heavy loads of hopelessness and despair away from our path. A realistic human being is to create simple yet thoughtful plans, and must be truthful in such pursuit. We learn from Buddhism that if a human being knows himself, he becomes free from the bondage of corporeal and unrealistic imaginary thoughts. When a human being becomes aware and realizes the actual value of knowledge, his unrealistic wishes and unfounded dreams will disappear. The strongest bond that holds us back is "not knowing". We are to understand that knowledge and ignorance are two different states that lead us toward different directions. A human being who chooses knowledge will not get lost in a world of attachments, but an ignorant one will, the destination of an unaware human being is nothing but wandering. A knowledgeable human being is free, more or less, from good and bad, the present and the future.

For example, we understand from Johann Fichte's (German philosopher, d. 1814) teachings that cognition is the essential basis for ethical acts and values. And ignorant individual cannot be beneficent. Every human being is free. No one can force people to harmonize their acts and deeds with beneficial principles. Only the knowledge of good and evil and their meanings can light the road to righteousness and make people beneficent.[36]

Scientists and geologists, who have investigated earth and classify its age according to traces of fossils and the age of metal, believe that our earth is several billion years old and is still traveling and journeying to an eternal perfection. But we may be cautious to accept this fact of a journey toward eternal—we may be afraid to lose our national, cultural, historical, hereditary frames of reference, or walk on the polished surface of destiny and travel in an unknown direction, with no destination, and end in eternal destruction.

There was a time when we felt ineffectual against natural forces like thunder, lightning, rain, earthquakes, darkness, the sea, and the sun. We thought that those forces were stronger than us. Consequently, we began to worship natural forces; we gave them appearance and called them gods and deities. We devoted ourselves to our creation; we sacrificed for Jupiter, Venus, Mars, Neptune, and Uranus, and sought help from these gods; we asked these gods to protect us against dreadful and unfortunate events; we begged them to grant our wishes and dreams. The history of humanity is saturated by the stories of these sacrifices; throwing our loved ones into the dreadful oceans and burning flames in order to calm the anger of those gods.

What we have forgotten, in the middle of all those unrealistic miraculous incidents, was the existence of the god of "self-confidence"; we forget that it is not the "human-made idols" that perform miracles, but the human beings' own self-confidence that leads to wonders. Those gods supported made-up tributes and celebrations amongst people. We can still find those kinds of traditions among tribes and societies. Primitive humans had no knowledge about natural forces and events and feared their effects. We did not know, so we created idols that suited the circumstances of our time, and we began and continued to worship and respect those idols. We counted on those idols as our own influential supporters. Time passed, people added more to those

---

[36] For more information on Fichte's views see Dan Breazeale, "Johann Gottlieb Fichte," *The Stanford Encyclopedia of Philosophy* (Summer 2018 Edition), Edward N. Zalta (ed.), URL = <https://plato.stanford.edu/archives/sum2018/entries/johann-fichte/>

traditions. But, in the middle of all these adventures, we should have realized our own merit, our own personal belief that was the creator of miracles. As we forgot and continue to forget our own excellence we add more colorful gods to our history of worship. And the god of personal belief; the god of self-confidence remained and remains forgotten. It is our personal belief; it is our own confidence that makes our wishes comes true. It is our own belief and faith that accepts our prayers, yet we have transferred this most important strength and force to the idols we, ourselves, have created.

But this god of confidence, who is the gatekeeper of awareness, is respected and worshipped less than other gods, since confidence is not set in a temple and cannot be objectified. But this does not change the fact that the strength and ability of this god is more than it appears. What is attributed to the gods is simply the miracle of a human being's belief and faith. The deep powerful voice of conscience, the truth of human nature, hidden behind those idols, continues to manifest itself. The voice of belief has been heard many times and through many voices.

Both barbarity and civilization have heard the voice of truth in nature, yet it is the pure soul that is willing to see and hear those signs. In other words, the ones who have the potentiality to understand will understand. It doesn't matter if we are devoted to and worship an idol, a statue or a tree. Whether we are primitives devoted to those idols, or if we are educated spiritual beings, truth will present itself, either from behind the stone idols or through an excellent soul, and will always lead the human civilization. The absolute existence has entrusted a human being with reality, yet so many layers of human beings' selfishness and egotism have covered such reality; and these veils have made it hard to recognize human merit from behind so many layers of disguise.

It is important to pay attention to what, for example, Xenophon (Greek philosopher, d. 354 BC) professes: that if horses and oxen could paint like human beings, then they probably would have painted their gods after their own images.[37]

---

[37] See James Lesher, "Xenophanes," in *The Stanford Encyclopedia of Philosophy* (Summer 2021 Edition), Edward N. Zalta (ed.), URL=https://plato.stanford.edu/archives/sum2019/entries/xenophanes/.

The unrealistic dictations and traditions of cultures and nations will take one to an imaginary and unrealistic far away goal; goals that are ambiguous and confused. Those unrealistic traditions lead an innocent or unaware human being towards an uncertain, unstable, vague, and superficial confirmation. And thus such a human being will worship the unknown and beg for help from a mysterious domain. Knowledge is essential in any pursuit. Probably this is what Spinoza refers to when he agrees that the more a self knows its capabilities and faculties, the easier it can organize itself and create discipline for itself; the more the self knows the discipline of nature, the easier it can abandon useless matter.

We are to agree that the propagation of the unfounded, fictitious and superstitious causes the inexperienced mind to wander for a while. Yet, every individual who has searched within himself will discover at least some simple and essential principles. These principles can dictate one's intentions.

Once we begin the journey on the road of understanding, we will become more aware of our own potentiality; the road towards reality will be more distinguished for us; yet this will not be the case if we were to merely observe the happenings.

COMMENTARY

Shah Maghsoud writes in his *Manifestations of Thought* that, "Scientific researches and discoveries are introductory works for any individual who seeks knowledge; since the core of knowledge lies within the nature and consciousness of the human being," and continues that, "A scientist sets his thought in his nature-self, and in a stable centrality within himself. If this centrality is infinite, then he or she can travel through a 360-degree circumference surrounding, through a progressive computation on the table of the existence. Though this scientist will never get to the edge of this surrounding, wherever he or she is, he or she conceives of peace and tranquility resulting from understanding the truth of nature and the nature of truth. Therefore, he does not confuse the appearances and dimensions with facts and reality of the Being; he looks at his hypothesis, not as finality, but as an introduction to knowledge."[1]

We have learned that the innate human curiosity and quest to study and understand the nature is entrusted to all; however, the question remains if the human mental faculty is capable of discovering the unchanging essence and facts of nature; if not, then where can the center of the human being's truthful understanding be, is human's understanding limited to dimensional realities, or is his understanding potentially limitless and so unbound by limitation, and, finally, is there any reality to things outside of human's mind?

The human being has employed the faculty of his mind discovering the laws of nature, together with his laboratory equipment that is perhaps a more precise extension of his mental faculty; but he is not limited to his mind, as he also has attuned his being to the beauty of nature and relied on his intuition and his heart's inspiration in creating

---

[1] Shah Maghsoud, *Manifestations of Thought*, trans. Nahid Angha, First Discourse, 7.

magnificent works of art, literature, monuments of civilizations and epic movements towards global justice and peace.

If we look into philosophical approaches, we learn that a group of philosophers, such as Plato, suggest that we are capable of a partial understanding of things, and can so partly learn about their fact-reality; or perhaps, "... of course the clear and certain truth no man has seen [...] 'however many things' the gods have made available to [humans] to experience"[2] as the Greek philosopher Xenophanes (c. 570-478 BCE) writes.

If we carefully study our own perception we see that what we perceive as the facts of the objects of perception differs from the actual reality and the fact of those objects themselves. What we see or think that we see depends on our physical health and mental state; if everything remains the same and nothing changes, we change nonetheless, and thus we perceive the same thing differently at different times.[3] These personal attributes and qualities subtly but continually contribute to the way we perceive our surroundings. The reality and the fact of the *what* of the outside world cannot therefore be truly perceived, Shah Maghsoud has emphasized in his writings.

If the dimensions dominating our mind were different, we would have perceived things and our surroundings differently. However our perceptions of our surroundings does not change the actuality of the elements, objects, and our surroundings.

If a human being relies only on mind-perception as a main source to unveil the mysteries of the universe, Shah Maghsoud suggests, then he may deprive himself from understanding the effects and hidden forces of the universe. Perception is a limited vehicle to lead a human being towards understanding the infinite and eternal.[4] Some philosophers have also suggested that the human mind is incapable of understanding

---

[2] See Lesher, "Xenophanes."

[3] While Plato argues that there must be an ultimate truth; Protagoras, on the other hand, offers a Subjectivist's opinion that any argument over right or wrong is only an opinion, nothing more; and "of all things the measure is Man..." Thus all experiences are relative to the person who is experiencing them. (See Joshua J. Mark "Protagoras," in the *Ancient History Encyclopedia*, 2009).

[4] Nahid Angha, *Negāh: Tahshi'-i-bar Padidihay-i fikr* (Tehran, Maktab-i-tariqat-Uwaiysi-Shah Maghsoudi Series, 1979.) 43.

anything beyond surface manifestations; and understanding reality, fact, and the abstract is beyond human mental ability. There is a sound logic in what Xenophanes (Greek philosopher, d. 475 BC) asks, "How much can any mortal being hope to know?" "Does truth come to us through our own efforts or by divine revelation?" "What role do our sense faculties play in the acquisition of knowledge?"[5] Or perhaps other group of philosophers, such as Protagoras (Greek philosopher, d. 411 BC) may have a point stating that "Of all things the measure is [hu]man: of those that are, that they are; and of those that are not, that they are not."[6]

For many philosophical schools, the knowledge of the real is the knowledge gathered by the intellect.

Should we consider "knowledge" (knowing things as they are) different from the perceptions of the senses since knowledge, in its abstract sense, remains stable and unchanging, while, as we noted, perceptions of the elements change? Thus, perceptual knowledge has no underlying generality, and so will not remain unchanging and stable. Perhaps we may refer to this kind of knowledge as information, or knowledge of the surface, Shah Maghsoud suggests. Since knowledge of the surface is only a partial understanding, and, our minds do not really and exactly perceive an object, but an image or a picture of that object. Even our own state of health and mentality contributes to the moment of our perceptions. *What* we perceive very much depends on *in what state of mind* and *how* we perceive it. What we imagine as being factual knowledge is more probably a short-lasting mental reaction and experience of the mind's own taste and creation.

Fact should not change, Shah Maghsoud emphasizes in his *Manifestations of Thought*; it should remain clear and unchanging, and its existence should remain doubtless. Emotions and affections we perceive when confronting a beautiful or unpleasant surrounding hide the reality and actuality of the "self-hood" of what is perceived. To expect emotion, perception, or sense experiences to give us a notion of

---

[5] Lesher, "Xenophanes."

[6] Mauro Bonazzi, "Protagoras," in *The Stanford Encyclopedia of Philosophy* (Fall 2020 Edition), Edward N. Zalta (ed.), URL=https://plato.stanford.edu/archives/fall2020/entries/protagoras/

what is permanent and fixed is irrational, as they are neither fixed nor permanent. Putting aside the philosophical ideologies that indicate that things exist within the human mind, we must admit that things will exist, whether or not there is a human mind. Our knowledge of them is but relative knowledge; and our perceptions of them do not change the actuality of the elements, of the objects.

We read in Spinoza's (philosopher, Dutch, d. 1677) philosophical doctrines, for example, that a human being attains his knowledge either through learning from others and believing in what he has learned; learning through his experience, the experience that most likely gives him a partial and subjective image of things; or he is learning through reason and understanding the relationship between cause and effect and thus will be "knowing a thing ... in the best way."[7] In some cases, a human being gains his knowledge through his own intuition. Would each learning process limit the outcome of the acquired information? Or is there any inherent knowledge within the very core of the human being apart from what he learns, experiences, reasons, or intuits? Doctrines Shah Maghsoud explains in his *Manifestations of Thought* to lead us to the unchanging center of understanding within the very corporeality of human system that holds an inherent knowledge of the existence.

· ON THE THEORY OF CAUSALITY ·

Philosophers have established theories, such as cause and effect, as a foundation for many of the philosophical theories of knowledge. Philosophers and scientists have given properties and qualities to this notion, and establishing rules based on this doctrine to adduce logical principles that theoretically dominate and govern the universe. However, when we examine this notion that has become the basis for our established logic, we learn, according to Shah Maghsoud, that "cause and effect" are, in fact, two principles reflecting each other, or two sides of the same coin differentiated by the language of logic, but not in the actuality of things themselves. Elements exist as they

[7] Nadler, "Baruch Spinoza."

exist; they are potentially the cause-effect of many other known and unknown (to us) potentialities that govern them and their relationship to other elements. They are what they are; they are not, however, words that we relate to them. What is "cause" or "effect" if not only our own relative perception of a limited space/time dimension of the actuality of being? This is especially true since we always have to think within the domain of space/time, and cause and effect are but the attributes of space/time. Can such a notion or any other term become the doorway to unveil the unchangeable knowledge of self-hood of things? Shah Maghsoud indicates that he doubts if civilization takes the inherently vague theories, or believes in the power of storage of words kept in the memory of books, as the foundation for an eternal knowledge. Illusion, imagination, and assumption are the foundations of many human achievements and mistakes, but they cannot direct one to the actuality of things, since they are like porters who "carry the unknown loads along long roads ...."[8]

Cause and effect may apply to the world of dimensions but have no generality or application in the abstractness of existence. Let's take "life" for example. Life is the very core of existence. It permeates the eternal and the infinite existence; presents itself in form and in formlessness; our knowledge of its formlessness and of its flow (in forms) is limited; we call life and its presentations by many names. Our theory of cause and effect does not apply to the very meaning of *life*. Life, by its very existence, is neither cause nor effect. It is not born from anything and its so called effect is nothing but its presentations in forms, inclusive of the essence and substance. We do not know or understand the absoluteness of life, but we refer to life's presentations by names and terms; we call one cause, and the other effect, theorizing that one name gives birth to the other, and we forget that both names are but the reflections of the same essence.

We can doubt everything, Shah Maghsoud theorizes, except the existence of our own being, or as Descartes (French philosopher, d. 1650) stated in his *Meditations*, "I am a being who thinks, and I have

---

[8] Shah Maghsoud Sadīq Angha, *Avaz-i-Kodayān*, trans. and commentary by Nahid Angha, *Psalms of Gods* (California: International Association of Sufism Publications, 1991) 10.

discovered this because of my own being." "[And] if I convinced myself of something then I certainly existed." "[No one will] bring it about that I am nothing so long as I think that I am something. So after considering everything very thoroughly, I must finally conclude that this proposition, *I am, I exist,* is necessarily true whenever it is put forward by me or conceived in my mind."[9] So it appears that an "important part of metaphysical inquiry therefore involves learning to think with the intellect. Plato's allegory of the cave portrays this rationalist theme in terms of epistemically distinct worlds: what the senses reveal is likened to shadowy imagery on the wall of a poorly lit cave; what the intellect reveals is likened to a world of fully real beings illuminated by bright sunshine."[10]

The human being exists, and is capable of understanding the minutiae of the existence, Shah Maghsoud states, but his *information* is relative. However, if the knowledge of "being" that is the very essence of the formed cosmos exists, then the human being must necessarily be aware of it. Every manifestation appears from and is based upon a fixed point of its actuality, and everything in this universe has its reality, and the center of eternity extends from the heart of the particle to the heart of eternity.[11] If we agree that every manifestation must rest upon a point of reference and that the center or the core of the element or the particle is actually the center and core of the universe, then to understand and fully know one centrality (unchanging center-point) would be equal to understanding the whole of the universe. Or as in the words of Leibniz (German philosopher, d. 1716) "[…] the *complete individual concept* contains all predicates true of a substance past, present, and future, the entire history of the universe can be read (if only by God) in the essence of any individual substance."[12] Perception is, however, a limited vehicle

---

[9] Lex Newman, "Descartes' Epistemology," in *The Stanford Encyclopedia of Philosophy* (Spring 2019 Edition), Edward N. Zalta (ed.), URL=https://plato.stnford.edu/archives/spr2019/enteries/descartes-epistemology/.

[10] Ibid.

[11] See Nahid Angha, *Negāh*, 42.

[12] Brandon C. Look, "Gottfried Wilhelm Leibniz," in *The Stanford Encyclopedia of Philosophy* (Spring 2020 Edition), Edward N. Zalta (ed.), URL=https://plato.stanford.edu/archives/spr2020/enteries/libniz/.

to lead a human being toward understanding the infinite and eternal.[13]

Shah Maghsoud suggests that it is the very "self" of a human being, a concentrated electromagnetic force, that understands its own self; everything else is a description of the "self" not its actuality. And, since every manifested self is rooted in its own core knowledge, then a human being can understand his own "self" through directing his concentrated energies toward a center-point of reference.[14] And the terms such as *cause and effect* lose their application since whatever is determined as effect or cause is but a presentation of its own essence.

For a human being who, according to the dictates of nature, has learned to rely on his senses and regard them as the doorway to knowledge, it is difficult to take a different step to build the foundation of his understanding. Knowing is the unveiling of the essential center of knowledge inherent within every particle, including humankind, Shah Maghsoud says. Every particle has a perfect knowledge of its own being, and so does every cell of human physicality; every organ of the human system knows its function perfectly—is there, then, any reason we think that a human being, the whole system, is deprived of the knowledge of its own self?

In his first chapter of *Manifestations of Thought*, Shah Maghsoud concludes that the conceptions resulting from external images, through terminologies, are just descriptions of the observer's momentary state of mind and mood. This knowledge is based on sensory appearances, not on the reality of the observed objects. A sensory observation will usually recall memories from our unconscious or conscious mind, is contributed to and accompanied by the association of ideas that will color our views. However, as we noted, the human being's mental acceptance interferes with the sensory appearances; it is impossible to perceive objects as they are. Therefore, external, superficial, sensory observations that the conscious mind photographs, gathers and analyzes according to its present qualities are made up and shall not be called knowledge; they are gathered by the senses to accumulate the

---

[13] Nahid Angha, *Negāh*, 43.

[14] This point ultimately leads to Shah Maghsoud's presentation of *'uqdah-i hayāti* (locus of life), his signature point, with a focus on the electromagnetic centers of the human system and their relationships with the cosmic energies.

storage of our memory; they are bound by the notion of space/time measurement. The absolute knowledge is unchanging and free from comparisons; it is inherent.[15]

And thus the very inherent knowledge is the cause of its own being and its effect is nothing but the presentation of its own self; and such does not rely on our logical explanations or limit by our own created terminology.

· ON FREE WILL AND HUMAN DESTINATION ·

Is a human being freely born into a destiny?

For centuries, human "free will" versus "predestination" has been a highly intriguing subject of philosophical inquiry. Philosophers have debated the relation between freedom and causality and its detailed implications as far as the limits of logic permit. To address these issues, a short review of the philosophical theories on freedom and causality may be important.

Mystics tell us that the essence (*juhar*—not relating to the philosophical debate over the *essence* and *existence* theories here) is the unchangeable core of a thing, its proper identity; while appearance or phenomenon consists of its changeable attributes, and how the essence manifests itself to a perceiver. In this sense, cause is labeled as the essence, with effect as its derivative. It is exactly the relationship between cause and effect, per se, that makes the alternative conceptions of free will and determinism/predestination difficult to grasp and identify. It is easy to imagine a temporal relationship, with cause appearing first in time and effect later, so that the senses would first perceive a cause, and then an effect; or senses experience an effect and then look for its cause. In actuality, the idea of cause and effect being perceptibly separable and subsisting in a temporal relationship is untenable, as [previously] noted; since the cause is, in fact, a carrier of the effect; the common belief that cause precedes effect is actually a confusing idea, according to Shah Maghsoud. Neither can precede the other in a non-dimensional system but only in a dimensional

---

[15] Shah Maghsoud, *Manifestations of Thought*, trans. Nahid Angha, First Discourse, 12.

time/space system. We perceive such a consecutive pattern because our logic mimics what our senses perceive. This relationship is our own understanding of a principle in the universe; or even, perhaps, a partial understanding of a partial principle in the universe. We lack a complete picture of the universe from which to adduce a complete understanding. If we add the subjects of soul and body, creation and creator, and free will and predestination to this incomplete picture of cause and effect, essence and appearance, then a factual understanding becomes more unattainable.

A human being may need to step a bit beyond his physical limitations, according to Shah Maghsoud, to understand how free will and predestination are intermingled and hold no meaning independently. Philosophical terms suggest ideas meant to understand the world of contingent possibilities; beyond such a world, they do not hold any accuracy. We also learn that the philosophers refined those suggested terms over time, adding their new explication to contribute and add to the volume of this great book of philosophy. And even though science gradually emerged from philosophy, it invented new terms and categories and claimed independence from philosophy, yet the underlying assumptions of the contemporary sciences remained based on the ancient suggestions of philosophy and its logic!

The notion of free will and predestination also brings us a range of philosophical debates: of the world based on a divinely predetermined organization where god has free will, while a human being does not; god precedes all creation, and the human being and his will are the effect of this First and Necessary Cause; god oversees all and the human being has power over small things; the human being has freedom only when he follows his intelligence and reason to make rational, moral choices; and so on. We also have to consider and comprehend the questions of reward and punishment within the notion of a free-willed and/or predestined world. Will knowledge of the facts be rewarding and the lack of it be punishment; will "knowing" help us better understand the matters of reward and punishment?

If we consider the subject of a creator, we may think of an active agent who is bound to the conditions in its creation. The first condition is the subject of movement, and the next is the subject of need or necessity; two hypotheses that have overwhelmed the world of ancient philosophy and have extended to generations of philosophical debates. The philosophical notions of "movement" and "necessity" are parallel, as the reason for movement is the necessity or the need to take an action. The relevant and the ancient questions in philosophy are: did the creator (God) take the tools to create its creation from outside existence, and by doing so, did it have to add something new to existence to fill the previous empty vacancy; or is existence simply one existence while non-existence does not exist! And there is nothing outside of existence, as there is nothing other than existence (then the philosophical debates over necessity and movement seem non-essential). If there is only one existence in its infinity (we cannot say there is not, because we do not know), then how can we process and treat the questions of creator and creation, the First Cause and its effect/creation? Perhaps the principal study is less on the creator/creation challenge but on a shift in focus on an absolute that manifests itself in forms; the core of the manifested forms, a Sufi ideology.

When we approach these philosophical inquiries and attempt to understand them fully, we may realize that these debates must be more complex than we may think. When confronting a decision, does a human being have free will in decision-making or is his choice bound to follow a predetermined destiny? Philosophical idealism may theorize that, since the human being is intelligent, he has the freedom to make a choice according to his intelligence. However, should we also consider one's inherited intelligence, cultures and times, laws and governing principles of the universe, the hidden energies and agencies in leading a human being in certain directions? We are born into cultures, time-eras, certain genes, social status, and more; would these elements direct our decisions, destinations, and inspirations? Haven't these elements that existed without our decisions, predestined our directions, our birth?

Another issue with the hypotheses of free will and predestination is the question of reward and punishment. How will understanding the essential factors of Being help us comprehend the meaning of moral reward and punishment; will "knowing" help us to better understand the matters of reward and punishment; since the question of free will and predestination brings us to a duality of a creator versus a creation; a rewarder and a rewardee. Philosophical theories fall into: those which assert that a Creator (not only divine but any cause of creation) produced and fashioned the creation and established fixed rules and laws for that creation; or that omnipotent Creator produced a creation but has also given his creation the freedom of choice.

In classical philosophy, Kant (German philosopher, d. 1804), for example, may suggest that if a human being acts in accordance with reason, he is therefore free; since the groundwork of practical reason presupposes freedom;[16] while Maeterlinck (Belgian poet, d. 1949) may suggest that the questions of free will and predestination are asked only within the limitation of human life, otherwise these questions have no place in the eternal existence, and writes that "Humanity up to this day has been like an invalid tossing and turning on his couch in search for repose; but therefore nonetheless have words of true consolation come only from those who spoke as though man were freed from all pain."[17] "Thither, in truth, is man led by his instinct, though he never may live to behold the long-wished-for to-morrow."[18]

To add to these narratives, some philosophers assume that matter/corporeality is substantial and thus real, while others give the precedence of greater reality to the soul (*ruh*), finer body; and a few recount mental or intellectual images and count them alone as real. Descartes, for example, may state that body (physical substance) and mind (mental substance) are different and independent from each other, but they interact with one another,[19] while philosophers like Leibniz, may debate that, "the mind and body can be said to form a union and interact insofar as the mind follows its laws, the body follows its laws, and they are in perfect harmony. The body and soul are not united to each other in the sense that Descartes had suggested, but the perceptions and appetitions of the soul will arise spontaneously from its own

---

[16] For more information, see Michael Rohlf, "Immanuel Kant," in *The Stanford Encyclopedia of Philosophy* (Fall 2020 Edition), Edwards N.Zalta (ed.), URL=https://plato.stanford.edu/archives/fall2020/enteries/kant/.

[17] Maurice Maeterlinck, *Wisdom and Destiny*, translated by Alfred Sutro (London: George Allen, Ruskin House, mdcccxcviii (1898) 7.

[18] Ibid. 8.

[19] For more information, see Lawrence Nolan, "Descartes, Ontological Argument," in *The Stanford Encyclopedia of Philosophy* (Spring 2021 Edition) Edward N. Zalta (ed.), URL=http://plato.stanford.edu/archives/spr2021/enteries/descartes-ontological/

stores and will correspond to the actions of the body as well as to the events of the world."[20]

In Sufism, the mysticism of Islam, thus in Shah Maghsoud's ideology, the human being is viewed as a manifestation of the abstract existence; and the abstract knowledge journeys in its manifestations, and thus necessarily a manifestation is united with its own core. While philosophical ideologies see the Divine as an entity perhaps separate from the human being, Sufi mystics see the human being as a manifestation of the Absolute, and thus capable of realizing one's essence, the core of one's being. For a Sufi, it is not enough to follow mind-reason, as reason may change; for a philosopher, reason is a sufficient vehicle. A classical philosopher may argue that when a seed is planted, whether there is free will or not, the seed is bound to grow, but a Sufi adds that a seed will grow only if there is harmony between the seed and its surroundings, including the hidden and apparent energies of the seed and the universe since a seed is not a separate and independent entity from the cosmic energies saturating the existence.

Shah Maghsoud points out that the abstract essence is abstract and not bound to the principles of qualities and quantities. However, since the abstract absolute manifests itself in the world of matter, confined energy, or nature, it manifests itself through forms and dimensions. Abstract is not understood through the form and shape it takes since only the Abstract understands the Abstract; however, the appearances and forms are not separated from the essence that manifests through them. Thus, in this regard, Shah Maghsoud disagrees with the philosophical idea of duality or multiplicity of reality or that the changing quality is the essence of an entity. Descartes, for example, relates that the "attributes are the essence of a thing, so the essence of mind is thought or thinking, and the essence of body is to be extended...."[21] To Shah Maghsoud, everything is a part of the essential rule of the eternal and infinite being, and we cannot divide existence into body and soul, abstract and possible, and give each a reality of its own, without

---

[20] Brandon C. Look, "Gottfried Wilhelm Leibniz."

[21] Noa Shein writes in her, "Spinoza's Theory of Attributes," in *The Stanford Encyclopedia of Philosophy* (Spring 2018 Edition), Edward N. Zalta (ed.), URL= https://plato.stanford.edu/entries/spinoza-attributes/

considering the unity of all that exists. Existence may manifest itself in dimensions, but no particle will stand independent from the wholeness of being, he says, for nothing is ultimately separable from anything else. Being may appear with many faces and in many manifestations to the eyes of a perceiver, but there is only one essential existence with multifaceted manifestations.

The philosophers, such as Kant, may emphasize the "principle of coexistence [...a] harmonious causal interaction between otherwise isolated, independently existing substances is possible only by means of God's coordination [....].[22] His suggestion seems to point to the idea that whatever relates to the natural world is phenomena and follows the principle of cause and effect. And, "the mind plays an active role in constituting the features of experience and limiting the mind's access only to the empirical realm of space and time."[23] Philosophers, such as Malebranche, introduce the doctrine of the "Vision in God" asserting that "we see all things in God, [a doctrine that] is intended as an account both of sense perception of material things and of the purely intellectual cognition of mathematical objects and abstract truths [emphasizing that,] God is the only genuine cause [... and] that we utterly depend on God in every way."[24]

We need to remember that we cannot follow the principle of cause and effect, which is the foundation of free will and predestination, repeatedly to finally arrive at the first cause as the cause of all effects as some schools of philosophy may suggest, for the book of cause and effect has no ending. Philosophers who emphasize the predestination of cause and effect (that the universe is like a clockwork mechanism) emphasize that determinism/predestination is a logical rule that everything is bound

---

[22] Eric Watkins and Marius Stan, "Kant's Philosophy of Science," in *The Stanford Encyclopedia of Philosophy* (Fall 2014 Edition), Edward N. Zalta (ed.), URL= https://plato.stanford.edu/entries/kant-science/

[23] Matt McCormick, "Immanuel Kant: Metaphysics," in the *Internet Encyclopedia of Philosophy*, nd. URL=https://iep.utm.edu/kantmeta/

[24] Lawrence Nolan, "Malebranche's Theory of Ideas and Vision in God," in *The Stanford Encyclopedia of Philosophy* (Spring 2022 Edition), Edward N. Zalta (ed.), Nolan, Lawrence. "Malebranche's Theory of Ideas and Vision in God." *The Stanford Encyclopedia of Philosophy* (Spring 2022 Edition), Edward N. Zalta (ed.), URL= https://plato.stanford.edu/archives/spr2022/wnteries/malebrabche-idea/

by. If so, then how do we respond to the question of ethics and morality where free will is a necessary foundation for choice; a foundation that serves the human being in his actions and moral decisions.

Our philosophers have proposed magnificent theories on the subjects of free will and predestination, as we have noted. Some have likened the world to a machine, and every part of it performs a job and has a responsibility, and everything *obeys* the rule of its being. A philosophical theory may suggest that the physical universe is like giant type-a machine with smaller type-a machines parts, some of which are the organic bodies of non-human animals and human beings.[25] And yet other philosophical theories may assert that, "only a substance can be uncompelled and free, [... and] that only God as the cause of itself can be attributed as being the one independent substance.... [and] thus what [people] conceive to be their free-will is only an infinitesimal way of conveying God's will."[26]

A few may even agree that "there is one infinite substance which can create anything due to its completely free will."[27] In other words, "God provides human beings with a will, and wills are intrinsically free. [...] If human beings restricted their acts of will to cases of clear and distinct perception, they would never err."[28] So as a matter of philosophical principle, the first cause gives the first movement to the world and all the parts and equipment fall into place and subsequently follow their own pace and motion; and the "thinking things, such as people, are free in nature"[29] even though a human being has also been considered

[25] For more information see Michael Wheeler, "God's Machines: Descartes on the Mechanization of Mind," in Husbands, P., Holland, O. and Wheeler, M., eds. *The Mechanical Mind in History* (MIT Press, Cambridge, Mass. 2008). For more information please see Michael Wheeler, *Reconstructing the Cognitive World: the Next Step*, A Bradford Book; 1st Edition, 2007.

[26] Rocco A. Astore, "Examining Free-Will Through Spinoza and Descartes," in the *Inquiries: Philosophy*, Vol. 8, No. 02, 2016, 1-21. For more information please consult: Benedict de Spinoza, *Ethics*, E. Curley, ed., (Princeton: Penguin Books, 1996).

[27] Ibid.

[28] See Hatfield, "René Descartes."

[29] Rocco A. Astore, "Examining Free-Will Through Spinoza and Descartes". Also please consult: R. Descartes. R. Ariew trans., *Discourse on Method* as found in *Rene Descartes: Philosophical Essays and Correspondence* (Indianapolis: Hackett Publishing Company, Inc., 2000).

as a part of this huge machine of the world; which of course, makes the human's freedom conditional, since a *part* has to follow the rule of the *machine*, whether or not he can choose good over evil remains a question. There are several difficulties with this conception of human freedom that are common to dualistic systems. If the human being is physically a part of this predestined machine of the world, how can he possess or exercise his intellect's, or mind's freedom of will? And who suggests the sense of goodness and wickedness, for we know that these notions are in part relative and so do not exhibit a universal aspect among everyone at all times. The meanings of goodness and wickedness change not only from one nation to another and from one time in history to another, but also even in the mind of any individual who grows older and judges actions in different ways.

Existentialism has turned these theories into its own dogma, asserting that existence precedes the essence and that the human being is responsible for his own actions and must recognize this responsibility. Thus, through the changing possibilities and relative values of life, one must constantly consciously choose an action for its own sake, instead of relying on any moral principles. Some may even say that when I realize that I have a choice in making decisions, and/or I am able to evaluate moral value and act upon my evaluation, then I have free will to choose and act. Others may say that the human being is the only animal with free will, and when he understands his free will, then he does not have to obey the rules of nature. This is an idea that leads us to ask: how can we separate the rules of nature from the rules of being? Can we ignore the influence of celestial waves and energies over our own lives? The human being is bound to obey the laws of being, and his free will is also another law and system that he follows. In other words, free will is a part of following the governing laws and principles of existence. However, the more one knows, the more one may expand his possibilities. For example, gravity is an unchanging law. Understanding this law helps the human being expand his knowledge of living well, understanding aerodynamics, and progress well when better understanding this law. The principle of gravity does not change, but our knowledge of it gives us greater possibilities (while relaying on that unchanging essential law). Anything we choose or do is a part of the greater law and codified system. Or, we may even say that, "the innermost nature [*Innerste*], the underlying force, of every representation ("presentation," "idea," or "mental image[30]") and also of the world as a whole is the will, and every representation is an objectification of the will...."[31] a doctrine closer to Shah Maghsoud's idea on free will, as we see later.

It would appear that the infinite existence manifests itself into the world of finitude through the most delicate computation by its own will; *its own will* is perhaps a set of unlimited unchanging principles permeating the core of all that exists, laws within its own laws. These unchanging laws are active and receptive at the very core of the particle, organic or non-organic. Will these unchanging laws define the human being's idea of free will or predestination? We should consider that a human being is existence in its limited form, necessarily inheriting all that exists: the active and receptive law, free and destined, according to Shah Maghsoud. Do we not have to choose using the faculties that we have been equipped with for choice? Can that choice then be called free? To what extent has the human being participated in his long journey of evolution that he now can participate in moral choices; and are the moral choices the *dictates* of times and cultures? The more the human being undertakes progressive development through the ladder of evolution, the more he learns of just how much lies beyond his control. Yet at the same time, he, himself, is a universal principle that will determine the road of the future generations of humankind. His inherent wisdom, knowledge, deeds, thought processes, moral or immoral actions, etc., are like small seeds planted in the history of humankind that over time will come to fruition, leading humanity to a destiny. Our history is an excellent example of such determinations. Our immune systems have developed extensively, our lifestyle, our longevity and health, our moral principles, our moral voice, our knowledge, our mental views have changed; we progressed thanks to the past generations' determinations.

---

[30] Robert Wicks writes in his "Arthur Schopenhauer," in *The Stanford Encyclopedia of Philosophy* (Fall 2021 Edition) that "Schopenhauer believes that the world has a double-aspect, namely, as "Will" (*Wille*) and as representation (*Vorstellung*). The German word, "*Vorstellung*", can be translated as "representation", "presentation," "idea", or "mental image." Edward N. Zalta (ed.), URL= https://plato.stanford.edu/entries/schopenhauer/

[31] Quotation relates to as Schopenhauer. See Mary Troxell, "Arthur Schopenhauer," in the *Internet Encyclopedia of Philosophy*, nd. https://iep.utm.edu/schopenh/

Shah Maghsoud writes that "Existence is self-controlled by its own determination, and the free will of the limited hypothetical particles and elements of the universe are, too, drawn on the infinite, unlimited circle of the laws and principles. [...] In this infinite universe, the magnetic waves between planets control the program and destiny of orbital arrangement; nowhere has been left out from these strong, influential dynamics. When we look at the planets and sparkles in the Milky Way, they seem to work independently with no connections or transactions with each other."[32] Yet none continues its journey without the pulls of the others.

"In the orbital atmosphere, the roaring and transacted waves lead lost, wandering and undecided huge planets to their destination. They compute and manage the universe with a very careful arrangement, but they seem so silent and quiet and the sky looks so quiet. But if a simple little substance, or atom, moves and displaces from its axis unexpectedly, it will take the whole universe to an unknown destination so that the existence of nature, as it is now, will be uncertain."[33]

These poetic theories tell us that we are connected no matter how ideologies are explained by our perceptions and comprehensions. There are plenty of unknown elements within nature. It is impossible to accept that the orbital disciplines, laws and systems have no influence on the way I live my life, the way I think, or on my being as a whole, Shah Maghsoud teaches. "I cannot accept the idea that a creature who comes into being from nature's womb, has been cherished by, and existed because of the existence of the nature [whose monumental and present being is the result of a long voyage] will disregard the natural laws in order to control the Nature [....]."[34]

In Shah Maghsoud's philosophy, predestination does not refer to the powerlessness of the human being or any entity in decision making, but rather states that a human being is capable of understanding the existing yet unchanging laws within laws in the universe; that all the elements of the universe are essential parts of these unchanging principles. It is here, according to his philosophical principles, that

---

[32] Shah Maghsoud, *Manifestations of Thought*, trans. Nahid Angha, 8.
[33] Ibid. 8.
[34] Ibid., 8.

understanding and knowledge of the governing principles of the existence becomes essential, as it gives the human being the possibility to walk wisely according to those laws. The human being is capable of such understanding because he is in harmony and balance with the greater universe, since he, too, is one of the existing laws of the universe.

A monotheistic view upholds the idea of the one and the only omnipotent living core of all that exists, the core and essence that is bounded by its own very principle; a principle that permeates all essence and manifested forms. Rules saturate the wholeness of being from the smallest particle to the largest galaxy. There is no creator (in its superficial term) but there is an abstract and absolute essence within the very being of forms, of dimensions, of manifestations.

If we can describe the existence as it really is, then there is no "other" than the existence to follow its own set rules; and the idea of predestination as a destiny-maker enforcing his destiny upon a destined, or the idea of free will suggesting a chaotic world of no rules and organization, lose their meanings and applications, states Shah Maghsoud. The realm of existence has unchangeable laws, very much like those of mathematics, where the rules of mathematics cannot essentially be referred to as predestined or free-willed. The only way to understand the reality of the abstract existence is to become free from the limitation of dimensions. As long as happenings, events, accidents, and possibilities are observed, then the cause and effect terminology applies. Our explanation of the existence and its free will or its predestination is a logical perceptional explanation of a human being; while the reality of the existence remains Absolute; an Absoluteness that exists without the need for *you* or *I*; *beginning* or *end*, *creator* or *created* form; since time/space is our definition of dimensions, and dimensions do not hold originality.

· ON HUMAN MORALITY ·

Long ago, perhaps in the late seventies, I read an article written by a psychologist philosopher who made an interesting observation. The article was printed in a local newspaper and was about a young boy who committed a crime and was subsequently sentenced to a few years in prison. The article was looking at this young boy's family history, his broken home, drinking problems, and illegal activities in his environment and neighborhood. All of those known factors, and those that remain unknown, worked together to direct this young boy toward a destiny. As John Hospers (American philosopher, d. 2011) writes, "Countless criminal acts are thought out in great details; yet the participants are (without their own knowledge) acting out fantasies, fears, and defenses from early childhoods, over whose coming and going they have no conscious control."[35]

Committing a crime may not be inherent in human beings, but there are agents and factors that may coalesce to direct someone onto the road toward criminality; then again, there are also those who take roads that may lead them to a different and peaceful direction. The factors that lead one may be traced back to the individual's genetics as well as one's susceptibility, acquired qualities, environment, cultures and times, etc. Some of those factors seem to be unchangeable and therefore outside the control of the individual such as DNA codes, genetics, birth into cultures, times, and environments. The notions of good and bad, however, are our own agreements for the survival of our communities. Nations destroy nations and lives in the name of democracy; religions slaughter innocent people in the name of savior-ship; the powerful steal from marginal communities in the name of development, and the list goes on. In other words, good and bad have no universalities; our definitions of moral actions are dictates of our cultures, minds, times, etc. In the vastness of culture, these terms of social agreements are manifestations of certain qualities, and so may become proper manifestations of the qualities they represent. However, neither moral nor immoral agreements have authentic meaning in the limitlessness of existence. They are our social agreements to protect our selves and our wellbeing.

Agreeing that everything that is part of existence follows its perfect

---

[35] John Hospers "What Means This Freedom?" in Sidney Hook, ed, *Determination and Freedom in the Age of Modern Science* (New York: SUNY Press, 1958) 114; John Hospers, https://depthome.sunysuffolk.edu/Selden/Philosophy/SE/handouts/Hospers.pdf, 357. Ron Yezzi, *Philosophical Problems: God, Free Will, and Determinism* (Mankato: G. Bruno & Co. 1993) 103-105. Also see Ron Yezzi, https://sites.google.com/site/rythinkingtourspi2/harddeterminism.

and suitable doctrine is not an opposition to the expectations of reward and punishment, as the rightful act is the act most desired by the community for its survival; yet one has to desire an act that is beneficial to the wellbeing of the human family; since ultimately, what a human being reaps needs to lead to the wellbeing of the entire human family, since the survival of a human being depends on the survival of humanity.

It is important to remember that the qualities that contribute to the making of an individual have evolved along the long pathway of life; such a journey of evolution has created the present complex being of an individual; a manifestation between the two worlds of the unknown: the past and the future. The existence of any being, according to Shah Maghsoud, is the profile of that being, an emergence from its abstract core to manifesting itself in dimensions, taking a long voyage of passing through galactic contractions and expansions, in the whirlpool of time and energies, to arrive finally on the footsteps of nature, being embraced by dimensions suitable for the life of the Earth; demanding to practice his freedom of choice!

Anthropologists tell us that beings survive according to their ability to overcome the forces of nature through struggle and cooperation, and thus through such a process, the fittest individuals and social groups survive. Nature tests her own creation, and after she is confident of her selections, she lets the fittest, according to her demands, survive. On this pathway of evolution, all the cosmic waves and energies and the whole of existence collectively determine the destiny of the being. The levels and stages of creation are not apart and separable from one another; rather, like the links of a chain, they are interlocked and work through their unity. Genes and molecules are the messengers that transmit the message of the past to the future in the most amazingly accurate way. The visible and invisible qualities of life transfer the information of past generations to their successors. We, ourselves, have received the mentality, physicality, and spirituality of our past ancestors, although often we may remain unaware of our inheritance. Hidden and apparent characteristics, endless qualifications and qualities, wills, desires, life and death, and many other factors contribute to the gestation of any being and then bring him forward to undertake the eternal voyage of the future. Any being is the mirror of his past and future. The seed of past lives has been handed down to us, to our generations, and the locus of this conversation is the tablet of our unconsciousness.

We are the work of artistic nature, who has gathered our present characteristics from many sources in the past and combined them with the most amazing calculation and elevated the result (the entity) to a level among the stages of her creation. She will take this system to any stage of her prediction and preserve it for any given future. She will not overlook any detail in making the gathering and scattering of this system. Indeed, nature preserves all the qualities of our ancestors and their way of life, whether they were one-cell or complex organisms, aquatic or terrestrial, knowledgeable or ignorant. Nature will pass on to us all necessary information through the complex systems of DNA, RNA, genetics and genomes, etc., and through us to any future generations.

Nature observes the governing law of heredity, which also includes our dominated environments and preferred lifestyles for all the members of her creation. Thus, not only one's whole past contributes and lives within the individual human being, whether potentially or actually, but also the entire nature. The scene of the waves of life of the past and the future of being, in which no memory will be obliterated or fade away, will be entrusted and delivered to the offspring of humanity. Nothing vanishes in the existence; for everything remains in waiting to be received by a suitable receiver. The receiver will reflect all those events and manifest them through the computed wave line and frequency observable by the suitable eye; at a very suitable time-dimension. Thus, *if our environment influences the genetics of our future generation, then it is important to pay attention to our moral decisions as well.* The human being is a complex and sophisticated creature; we practice compassion and kindness, and we practice greed and cruelty; we honor heroes of humanity, and we celebrate the villains; we value life and mourn its loss, and justify our brutality; we fall in love and our romantic love stories saturate our music, poetry and storytelling, yet we justify our revenge and prejudice. On one hand, a human being devotes his entire life to ease the pain of another, and at the same time, he develops the most advanced weapons of mass destruction. All these moral choices will be entrusted to our future generations. *So we are to evaluate the benefits and the destructive power of our age and the seeds we plant for future generations to reap.*

Shah Maghsoud has remained among the spiritual leaders to advocate and support social change and human rights; he expressed his political views in many of his writings. Education, peace, morality, the environment, and individual rights were among his chief concerns. The knowledgeable people have contributed immensely to the advancement of civilizations and peacefulness of our lives, he says; thus it becomes the responsibility of a noble society to not only improve its educational system but also encourage its learned to take the frontier of knowledge to the highest possibilities for the sake of peace. The value and honor of any nation depend on the number of its educated people; as they remain the wealth and the asset of the nations. It is the responsibility of governments to open the doors of education for all if we are to improve the conditions of living for the human family, to foster individual progress, to open the door of new frontiers of science, to expand our space journey, to advance agriculture in our villages, and/or ultimately offer our future generations and our environment better and morally improved living conditions. We cannot ignore human potentialities and overlook the energy of our youth and future generations; it is education that promises the survival of human civilization, not the advancement of tools of destruction.[36] Shah Maghsoud suggests that we are to correct and improve our inner and outer attributes and qualities, otherwise, the past we bequeath to the next generation will be shameful.[37]

Mir Ghotbeddin writes in his *Destination: Eternity* that since nothing will vanish into space, thus no matter how far the light wave travels from its center, it will always be observable by suitable receivers. The same is true for our actions and deeds of goodness or wickedness, servitude or treachery, friendship or enmity, hidden or apparent, he says. They all are carried away by the quickest wings of light into infinite space and are handed from wave to wave into eternity, written by the hand of the great writer onto the sensitive and mysterious pages of creation by the illuminated wave-lines. They will be so deeply engraved on the existence that nothing can erase them, and so they will remain, ready

---

[36] Nahid Angha, trans., *Manifestations of Thought*, 18-19.
[37] Ibid., 21.

to be reviewed at a proper time.[38] We also read in the "Reflection, Memory and Selfhood in Jean-Paul Sartre's Early Philosophy", "that as a young man he [Sartre] thought of his life as an 'oeuvre', that is to say, '… a series of works related to each other by common themes and all reflecting [his] personality.' [… his past] 'rose against a background of a life' as this very life 'was a rosette-like composition wherein beginning and end coincided: maturity and old age gave meaning to childhood and adolescence' […] life was 'a tapestry-frame to be filled' […]"[39]

Philosophers may agree that all the particles of the universe, including the human being, have their own memories, and their manifestations are the pictures of the past and present leading to the future. It becomes important that we remain cautious of the actions we take and the road we walk on, whether we are free or pre-destined, as Sartre writes, "an act is free when it exactly reflects my essence"[40] an action, free or not, is embodied deeply in the very core of one's being; as "[…] authentic choice stems from the fact that when I commit myself to my 'fate' I do so 'in and with my 'generation,'"[41] says Heidegger (German philosopher, d. 1976). So in this regard, the waves of my life, or any being for that matter, can be viewed at any time as my history dictates.

As a matter of fact, the book of the destiny of any particle is that particle itself, and the position of any particle in the universe is like a word in the book of existence; so that whoever has the necessary insight may read this book. And, if the unchanging laws of the universe are visible to the eye of the discoverer, then so are the life, actions, and thoughts of a human being to a susceptible observer.

As we receive from the timeless past, we also transfer to the timeless future. We cannot change the past, but we can understand the principles of being and adjust ourselves accordingly. Nature has equipped us to acquire knowledge, and the fittest to survive is the one who knows

---

[38] Mir Ghotbeddin Muhammad Angha, *Az Janin Ta Janan*, 2022, 148.

[39] Lior Levy, "Reflection, Memory and Selfhood in Jean-Paul Sartre's Early Philosophy," in *Sartre Studies International* (Berghahn Books, Vol. 19, No. 2) 97-111.

[40] Jean-Paul Sartre, *Being and Nothingness*, trans. Hazel E. Barnes (Washington Square Press; Original ed. Edition, August 1, 1993) 81.

[41] Steven Crowell, "Existentialism," in *The Stanford Encyclopedia of Philosophy* (Summer 2020 Edition) Edward N. Zalta (ed.), URL= https://plato.stanford.edu/entries/existentialism/

more and is better able to apply his knowledge to his survival, and his survival depends on the survival of nature and her inhabitants.

So, we arrive at this point: that the traces of the human being's footprints are marked on the roads of life, proportional figures and forms are always reviewable for the rational individual. At each level of existence that they appear, they carry the realities of their past. Action and reaction are the two impressions of the deed. Shah Maghsoud gives us this example: if a gardener forgets to water a plant, let's say in the third month of spring, this neglect will gradually show itself in the yellow faded leaves after a month or two; no compensation will be useful in amending the damages of the past.

One thing is certain: the world of dimensions is traveling from an eternal unknown point (unknown to humans) to another eternal unknown point, with no delays or stops. The human, too, is taking part in this journey, marking his impressions along this mysterious path. His deeds, thoughts, acts and imagination develop form and shape, apparently and inwardly; his present state is the center of his history and the introduction to his future journey. Humanity's physical and spiritual life, harmonious with the passing of time, is reflected in the face of existence. None of our past physical and mental happenings will be eliminated and forgotten; our steps are already imprinted upon the book of Being.

Every sound has its own characteristics and remains on a special wave line, and is received by a susceptible receiver; like those black and white reflections of a film appearing on the space between the origin and screen. It seems as if pictures have only natural form in their origin and destination (screen), whereas those reflected qualities, compositions and pictures, are also present in the space between the origin and the screen. If we look closely, we will see that those are particles, atoms, molecules, waves and metaphysical energies that make up natural figures. This eternal presentation, which appears differently in different stages of existence, is the appearance of that natural reality that is somehow visible to the human when it coincides with his senses. At the present time, we have printed and impressed our physical past and its consequent qualities on a special time-wave; they are present in the notebook of memory and the wrinkles of our brains, doctrines that Shah Maghsoud so masterfully presents in his writing.

The human beings who understand these chains of inheritance practice praiseworthy deeds, thoughts and purposes. A wise human being leads humanity to a praiseworthy direction by his own example.

Then, what is the role of human societies in providing peace and stability for humanity? Shah Maghsoud has often emphasized that peace, harmony, and stability are fundamentals in human life and the life of the natural world. So it becomes of the utmost importance for a human being to understand how he is presented in this existence, so he is not withered away, directed to wastefulness. The image of the fire is fearful only for the one who has flammable elements; otherwise, fire will not change the essence of the nonflammable. Moral and ethical teachings and their instructions are set to lead a human being toward peacefulness; and away from destruction and misery for the earth and its inhabitants.

So "[t]here comes a moment in life," [Maeterlinck] says, "when moral beauty seems more urgent, more penetrating, than intellectual beauty; when all that the mind has treasured must be bathed in the greatness of soul, lest it perish in the sandy desert, forlorn as the river that seeks in vain for the sea."[42] Moral principles are human codes set to promise the survival of all humanity, during time-eras and within cultural sets. Even though the meaning of good and bad conduct may change as we change, their destination remains the same: one leads to survival, the other to destruction, and all are bound by the visible and the invisible rules of the existence.

· ON FINITE AND INFINITE ·

It is no coincidence that our term "world" in its broader sense, encompassing all that may be experienced or understood, also refers to our planet earth. Throughout the world's history, the majority of humankind has identified the frontiers of knowledge with those of geography; and most of us are content to live in the physical world and some wish to know no other. Yet even the advances of science in the past and present centuries have neither altered understanding of knowledge

---

[42] Maeterlinck, *Wisdom and Destiny*, xiii.

nor expanded our view of the nature of the "world." Astronomers have probed the vastness of the universe only to realize the insignificance of the planet we inhabit yet we still see this universe as no more than a backdrop to our affairs, which we pursue without giving our place in it a second thought.

Astronomers have pointed out that it is realistic to assume that there exist planets similar to our earth both in nearby and in far distant galaxies. Although in the immensity of the universe it might be a rare coincidence to find a planet with exact qualities similar to our own, it remains not an impossible assumption. Now, if we were to take such an assumption as a possibility, then there might likewise be countless beings similar to ourselves living on those planets; individuals who also search for the reality of the existence, imagining themselves to be the only intelligent beings in the universe to question eternity. How vast and extensive could the knowledge of each one of these beings be in comparison to that of the existence? How far could the boundaries of their and our understanding extend? How limitless can human knowledge be; an individual human being residing in the small planet of earth that Carl Sagan (American astrophysicist, d. 1996) called the blue dot, at the edge of the Milky Way?[43]

Even though the goal of science is to discover and understand the universe, science cannot ultimately show us the shortest path to attain knowledge in this limitless existence.

When we look up at night at the heavens and see the light of the stars that shine so beautifully and gracefully we should remember that it was only a few decades ago that we could not believe that these stars were worlds that followed their own destiny. Even with our present knowledge we still cannot see them as giant planets and galaxies moving in accordance with their own directions. If we really could see the grandeur that surrounds the world we live in, then we would begin to question the importance of the limited knowledge that we have acquired; we would ponder on our relationship with this immense existence; we would carefully evaluate our significance or lack of it to this great universe. Our arrogance would be transformed into the deepest awe and we might begin to ask if there is any chance of understanding the

---

[43] For more information see: https://www.planetary.org/worlds/pale-blue-dot

meaning of infinite, that mystics so adamantly talked about, with such magnificence and beauty, so long as we are limited by nature. Yet at the same time I see the possibility of such unification, of such awareness, since, for myself, "I" am the universe, a living universe, as Shah Maghsoud has emphasized in his teachings so many times. The universe exists because I exist, and if there were no I, there would be no universe, it is ultimately the finite who has the possibility of understanding the infinite, the finite manifestation that is so deeply rooted to its essence, to its absoluteness. Even should the existence exist without me, I would neither know nor care as "I" could not be aware of such an existence to contemplate. But if for myself "I" am the universe, where does this dual notion of separation and unity come from?

Thinkers over time have categorized knowledge into two classes: limited knowledge acquired through sense perceptions and experiences, and unlimited knowledge of the ultimate and absolute reality; knowledge that resides in the stable factuality of that which exists. Our relative knowledge, as we all know so well, is founded upon our daily experiences that are personal to ourselves; it will not illuminate the path toward factuality or what we call the "reality" of anything. This kind of information should never be taken for the finality of human knowledge since it is not reliable. Similarly, the information of scientific findings is always subject to revision and restatement. The reason lies in the necessity of their very contingency, and the fact that the more we learn the more we review our previous and often tentative information as we attempt to advance our understanding. Throughout history, whenever a scientific truth was thought to be final, subsequent discoveries have revealed its transient and contingent value.

Let us begin to study the small universe called the human being, and find out how the "intelligence" within this system programs and follows its creation. We learn that our body consists of organs which each function separately as well as cooperatively with one another to maintain the survival of the human organism. The harmony of the whole is ensured through the genetic information carried within each cell, information sufficient not merely to replicate the cell but indeed the entire organism.

A gradual birth of the DNA, where each molecule plays a precise and well-defined function, is still one of the mysteries of life remaining to be discovered; chromosomes so magnificently pack the presence of DNA in the nucleus of a cell, pass along the history of the existence to an individual to inherit and to offer; safekeeping the uniqueness of each inheritor so the individuality and exclusivity of a recipient remains intact; and every day we learn more about the birth of life. And, so life is born through the cooperation of chromosomes, yet each chromosome must complete its mission before another chromosome begins its multiplication. It seems that this innate knowledge of life has its roots established well before the actual birth of the living cell. How do these chromosomes cooperate with and understand one another; is there an exchange of intellectual wave-energies between them; do they exchange energies that speak their language? Where does the intelligence of life reside, an intelligence that programs everything from the small cell to the entirety of the human body and not to overlook the existence of galaxies? Everything is so perfect in its function; all live within a harmonious system of cooperation and incorporation; and all walk within the boundary of corporeal principles. Every movement within the smallest particle follows a universal rule to fulfill its functions, yet every move is suitable to the element moved and follows its own destiny. Everything follows this most organized chart in existence. We may gradually learn its rules but we cannot change them. And indeed, our measure of the most advanced scientific discovery is that which mimics and follows these predestined rules the most closely.

Do we not carry within ourselves the unchangeable law of existence, are we not an organized chart of that intelligence, can I really overlook the existence of the Existence within? Human being has searched for an ultimate understanding of his universe. His senses developed a relationship of labor and energy between himself and his surroundings, and such cooperation has advanced the conditions of life for all humanity. Among the individuals who, because of their sensitive and searching characters, have advanced this relationship are laboratory scientists, Shah Maghsoud indicates. These individuals have made great contributions towards our understanding of the laws of the universe. They have well-marked their being upon the pages of human civilization.

Apart from these individuals we encounter another type of discoverers: the mystics. They, too, speak of knowledge and discovery, but on a different level. What they introduce is stable and permanent, less subject to revision but open to a greater understanding. They are steadfast in their teachings and announce universality in their message; they teach an understanding of the ultimate reality of the Self; and the knowledge they introduce is based on the illumination of the heart, and the enlightenment of the mind. This is what Suhrawardi (Persian mystic, d. 1191) has so beautifully taught that: once the soul is illuminated by the rays of the divine light, it would reach the glory and throne of the Absolute sovereignty.

Those teachers talk about the knowledge that illuminates and enlightens rather than simply passing along information; they talk about a light that lit the path towards a destination. In other words, the actuality of knowing, Shah Maghsoud indicates, is to be present in that factual knowing. A knowledgeable person will find his way into the depth of the actuality of knowledge; and thus discover the fact as it is, not as it is imagined, reasoned, or assumed. If we are to establish knowledge that is not founded upon doubt, then we are to seek knowledge through other ways than the senses and human-made logic. It does not mean we choose one over the other; but we are to be conscious of the road we are taking, and to the destination we are heading to; as ultimately "Consciousness essentially is only awareness, an attention to what is given […]."[44]

Shah Maghsoud indicates that the knowledge that leads towards discovering that which is permanent is based on the knowledge deeply rooted in existence itself; a knowledge that is infinite and actual; not the information gathered, but the knowledge discovered.

In his teachings, Shah Maghsoud suggests that understanding the reality of a human being, the core of one's own existence, begins from understanding one's own self as a doorway to understanding the greater reality. He emphasizes that embarking on a journey of self-knowledge is available for all human beings, yet not everyone will embark on such a journey. We also read in the principal philosophy of Santayana (Spanish philosopher, d. 1952) of the same notion that, "Shaping one's

---

[44] Herman Saatkamp and Martin Coleman, "George Santayana," in *The Stanford Encyclopedia of Philosophy* (Fall 2020 Edition), Edward N. Zalta (ed.), URL= https:// plato.stanford.edu/entries/santayana/

life to enhance [one's] spiritual, fleeting moments, extending them as long as is practical, is one of the delights of living for some people, but it is certainly not a goal for all, nor should it be."[45] There are those who search beyond knowledge of the temporary; they are eager to connect and unveil the essence of what is permanent. It is here that we are to become aware of our own reality; or as Marcus Aurelius (Roman emperor and a Stoic philosopher, d. 180) writes in his *Meditations*, "Look inwards. Don't let the true nature or value of anything elude you"[46] and that includes understanding the "I," the very "selfhood."

We learn from Shah Maghsoud's teachings that to embark on the journey of awareness one is to begin from understanding the "I" of one's self to be able to advance to understand the absolute "I" of the existence. For example, in his *Nirvan*, a metaphorical tale of "circular journey of return," the traveler, any aware human being for that matter, will gradually unveil the universe within: a universe that becomes the platform from which the journey of awareness of understanding the absolute begins. Shah Maghsoud teaches that a human being is capable of understanding "the Absolute" within the confinements of the space-time dimension. Perhaps the greatest human discovery is to understand that Unity: the union of the seen and unseen,[47] when "the herald of hope echoed in the infinite existence that: there is no non-existence and there is only one divine unity,"[48] it is there that one understands the meaning of the union of finite and the infinite.

To reside at the essence of knowledge is knowledge. The traces of images that cover the reality of knowledge impede human beings in their search for understanding. And so the mystics instruct their students to purify the mind and self from all other than reality. It is a good reminder that the "I"—the human self—exists, and exists in a defined dimension, having his own defined space in time within this boundless universe and its galaxies, and declares: "I am who I am, the

---

[45] Ibid.

[46] Marcus Aurelius, *Meditations*, trans. Gregory Hays (New York: Modern Library, 2003) 69.

[47] A reference to, "Wherever you look is the face of God," the absolute reality, Qur'an 2:115.

[48] Shah Maghsoud Sadīq Angha, *Nirvān*, trans with commentary by Nahid Angha (California: International Association of Sufism, 2021) 14.

one and only." If there is no continual connection with the absolute, then how can the "I," the absoluteness of "life," continue to exist within the majestic yet galactic energies of the cosmos, each declaring its own individuality; the absoluteness of "life" is momentarily confined in dimensions yet it never dies. Or as Angelus Silesius (German mystic, d. 1677) writes:

> In the Center everything is seen
> Stand at the center point—instantly shall appear
> All that befell or now befalls, in Heaven and here.
> [...]
> Time is eternity
> Eternity is one with Time,
> Time with Eternity, and hence
> Indifference between them lie,
> Thyself dost make the difference.[49]

However, whatever is temporary will return to temporary and whatever is Absolute remains Absolute; and so:

> I give back to the earth what the earth gave,
> All to the furrow, none to the grave,
> The candle's out, the spirit's vigil spent;
> Sight may not follow where the vision went.[50]

· ON BIRTH AND DEATH: THE IMAGES OF CHANGE ·

Death is an evolutionary and developmental part of being, Shah Maghsoud writes. Birth and death are but two reciprocal phenomena that may be understood as the stages of existence. Otherwise, existence is an absolute whole that encompasses all stages of its manifestations.

Death is among the most fascinating subjects that have attracted

---

[49] See Sacred Texts: Christianity Angelus Silesius, *VIII: TIME AND ETERNITY*: https://www.sacred-texts.com/chr/sil/scw/scw08.htm

[50] Jennie, "The Poet's Testament" George Santayana, 2015: https://wordsfortheyear.com/2015/04/01/the-poets-testament-by-george-santayana/; also see George Santayana, *The Poet's Testament: Poems and Two Plays* (New York: Charles Scribner's Sons, 1953).

the attention of scientists, philosophers, and mystics alike. Everyone speaks or thinks of death at some point and understands it according to one's own intellectual possibilities and one's own community.

Death is considered the finality of whoever traverses the pathway of life; and evolutionary journey to the "great beyond," *wherever that is*; a dissolution within the law of universal evolution. Camille Flammarion (French astronomer and author, d. 1925) so masterfully asks these questions in his book, *Death and Its Mystery: Before Death*: "Are we merely ephemeral flames shining an instant to be forever extinguished?"[51] "Shall we never see again those whom we have loved and who have gone before us into the Great Beyond? Are such separations eternal? Does everything in us die? If something remains, what becomes of this imponderable element—invisible, intangible, but conscious—which must constitute our lasting personality? Will it endure for long? Will it endure forever? Are we to die wholly?"[52]

From the beginning of life on earth, death has been accepted as an undeniable fact, the finality of entities, a disappearance into the realm of beyond. When we examine the process of dying, we understand that birth and death exist in a deep and unbreakable relationship. Birth ends in death, and death, in turn, supports life and clears the way for new generations. Yet, we learn about birth more quickly and more simply than we do about death. Birth is a visible process of life; we have time to study its process and outcome. Death has remained a mystery to us; life suddenly breaks and we lose our connection to the process of death. We develop a physical and visible relationship with the child born, but we lose that apparent and physical relationship with one who passes away. For the one born, we see its growth and development; for the other, we see no more. The visibility of birth makes it more accessible to study, while the invisibility of death makes it difficult to investigate. We are familiar with the boundary of birth, and we lack familiarity with the realm of death. It is also important to note that we are as unfamiliar with the before of birth as we are with the after of death. Before birth refers, of course, to the life of an entity

---

[51] Camille Flammarion, *Death and its Mystery: Before Death*, Volume I, trans. E. S. Brooks (Charleston, South Carolina: Nabu Press, 2010) 3.

[52] Ibid. 21.

before it is conceived; we know nothing about "life" before conception.

A human being is born and dies between these two stages of the unknown, Shah Maghsoud points out in his *Manifestations of Thought*. One is the past, he writes, that lies before conception, and the other is the unknown future of that corporeal life. It is clear that the more we learn about these two unknown realms, the more confident we will become in understanding the reality of life that lies between these two realms. In fact, it is the understanding of these two stages that will help us solve the puzzles of birth and death. It is the unknown realm of the past that participates in the birth of the present, and it is through the unknown door of death that the present takes its final stand and disappears into its destiny. Biologists and anthropologists may inform us that suitable elements have assembled and established the complex system called the human being. For science, the foundation of this system is chemical, mineral, and other known or unknown substances of nature. These elements and substances that existed on the earth, whether in its soil or atmosphere, visible or invisible, brought about the advent of life and so that of humankind. Scientists attempt to solve the mystery of life through a study of inanimate and living things.[53]

What does remain after death, if anything? Whatever breathes, eats, and digests possesses chemical and physical qualities; therefore, it is constructed and will scatter. In/animate objects are formed, built, constructed and will be dissolved. Both the whole organism and its particles eat and are eaten; they eat to be born and are eaten to regenerate. Each death is a beginning of a birth, and birth is the beginning destined to death. If there were no breathing, absorbing, and digesting, the manifestation of life would have been other than what we now see.[54]

We have learned that an organism continues its life through preserving and spending its energy and protecting itself from the destructive energies around itself. If the human mechanism does not continue to preserve itself, it will face destruction and natural scattering, ashes to ashes and dust to dust. The organism survives so long as it can continue in its collaboration between matter (condense energy) and energy with its surroundings. Since "living organisms are open systems, and

---

[53] Nahid Angha, *Negāh*, 130.
[54] Nahid Angha, *Negāh*, 132.

so must receive energy and materials from outside themselves, and are not therefore limited by the Second Law of Thermodynamics (which is applicable only to closed systems in which energy is not replenished)."[55] Any substance, food, energy, chemicals that enter the body of the organism must change and be digested to become suitable food energy so that the organism survives. The cells of the living organism are constantly in cooperation with the attractive and repulsive energies of the universe—the energies that take responsibility for the organism's life, and through their wave-frequencies trace the image of life on the tablet of existence in the most fascinating cooperation and harmony. Death comes as the result of the imbalance in this equilibrium of life, and, perhaps, a lack of harmony between all those forces (receptive and digestive) in the cells, Shah Maghsoud states. Influences from hidden and apparent, suitable and unsuitable energies create environments and conditions for an organism; these influences continue until the organism's death and perhaps even beyond. Death arrives at its suitable time, and when it occurs, cells undergo a drastic change.[56] This process is what Shah Maghsoud has referred to as condensation and expansion, a process that continues in the universal evolution where every stage is born from the death of another stage.[57] Mir Ghotbeddin Muhammad writes in his *Az Janin Ta Janan* that, "death of the body comes to us when old cells cease to be replaced by new ones; and the body will disintegrate; [...] yet that eternal "I," what we may call the soul, remains eternal. This is a reality that we do not see with the eyes of the head, but with the eyes of the heart, as the Qur'an (53:11) reads: the heart does not falsify in what it sees."[58]

One important note is that even though the whole living system of the human being will die, the chemical substances in him will not; instead, they will gather, transform, and scatter. In other words, the

---

[55] For more information see The Physics of the Universe: Alexander Oparin, https://www.physicsoftheuniverse.com/scientists_oparin.html; Alexander Oparin, *The Origin of Life on Earth* (New York: Dover Publications, 1965); Sidney W. Fox, "Aleksandr Oparin, Russian biochemist," in *Encyclopedia Britannica*; https://www.britannica.com/biography/Aleksandr-Oparin (nd).

[56] Excerpts from Nahid Angha, *Negāh*, 136.

[57] Excerpts from *Negāh*, 137.

[58] Mir Ghotbeddin Muhammad Angha, *Az janin tā janān*, 1984, 40.

human being in his present form is composed of cells that have been gathered from the elements of nature to form his colony, his organism. After living as a single entity, this system will scatter and return to its natural origins. So, the question remains, is "ashes to ashes, dust to dust" the finality of a human being? Maeterlinck in his *The Great Secrets,* "Would this illimitable mass, consisting of the total sum of all cosmic matter, including the etheric and all but spiritual fluid that fills the fabulous interstellar spaces, occupy the whole of the space, finally and eternally congealed in death, or would it float in a void more subtle than that of etheric space, and henceforth subject to other forces?"[59]

Death is not a gateway through which one passes to final destruction and nonexistence, but rather birth and death are the sequences of waves that constantly occur one after the other. Our body renews itself. Even though DNA may not change, the cell itself changes, or rather is replaced by a newer cell; this is yet another cycle of this constant and eternal flow of death and birth.

So, are we a "… thinking atom, borne on a material atom across the boundless space of the Milky Way, […] insignificant in soul as […] in body…[?]"[60] What does remain after death, if anything? Mystics have answers to this question, yet science has to find out if the electromagnetic energies stored in the human being die with him; if not, what happens to that storage of collected energy?

"The brain is a wonderful organ," writes Mir Ghotbeddin Muhammad, "which coordinates the body and serves as a receptive organ for inspirational energies. […] However, spiritual understandings are of different nature. These truths can only be understood if the profound guidance of "know thyself" which has been the single most important goal of seekers since before the Temple of Delphi was built, can be understood and acted upon. Truth gained through the optic nerve and the brain is of a different magnitude than that apprehended through the subtle organs."[61] He writes that every being will harvest whatever he has sowed

[59] Maurice Maeterlinck, *The Great Secret,* trans Bernard Miall (London: Methuen & Co. LTD, 1922) 73. Quoted from "Sanyatta Nikaya;" Vol. II, fol. 110 and 119.

[60] Camille Flammarion, *Death and its Mystery: Before Death,* Volume I, trans. E. S. Brooks (Charleston, South Carolina: Nabu Press, 2010) 3.

[61] Excerpts from Mir Ghotbeddin Muhammad Angha, *Az janin tā janān,* 2022, 47.

and [will return] to the utmost of his essential qualities. Otherwise, if as Materialist philosophers (philosophical doctrine professing that everything results from material interactions) believe, that a person passes through the hardship of life to end in final destruction, then we really should question this creation: all the perfect systems of the universe's laws and intelligence, advancements in civilizations, scientific discoveries, and indeed all the fundamental and most magnificent principles of the universe and creation must seem to be useless practice and childish games. From the materialist point of view, the system of creation could be likened to an unconscious and ignorant farmer who plants his field out of whim, lacking any special intention, and then forgets his harvest, so that the result of his labor that should be the most important part of the farming comes to naught. Such an allusion clashes with the carefully computed system of universe even insofar as science knows it, a system that seems further filled with wisdom and intelligence that expands particle to the galaxies.[62]

Death is a quality of the world of possibilities so that whatever is gathered under the rules of nature will be scattered under the same rules. We describe these stages as birth and death when we consider them as the stages of creation, but what remains unchangeable in this journey is the abstract essence that is the main core in the stages of creation; the absolute knowledge that journeys with its presentations of the stages of life.[63] That eternal essence (the absolute) remains in the depths and at the surface; it will not perish. Persisting through finite changes, its form may be transformed from one face to another, but nothing can be added or taken away from the existence of its absoluteness. The "I" of the existence; the "I" of the being remains. "When all the other gods are no more than disappearing names," says Max Müller (German philologist, d. 1900) in his *The Origin of Religion*, quoted in Maeterlinck's *The Great Secret* that, "there are left only the Atman, the self, and Brahma, the objective self; and the supreme knowledge is expressed in these words: '*Ta Twam, Hoc Tu*': 'That is you'; your true self, that which cannot be taken from you when all disappeared that seemed for a time to be yours. When all created things vanish like a

---

[62] Excerpts from *Destination: Eternity*, chapter four.

[63] Excerpts from Nahid Angha, *Negāh*, 137.

dream your true ego belongs to the Eternal Self: the Atman, the personality within you is the true Brahma: that Brahma from whom birth and death divided you for a moment; but who receives you again into his bosom, so soon as you return to him."[64]

If a human being ponders on the mysteries of the universe, he has no other way than to build upon the understanding of his own self. And indeed, the human being himself is one of the wonders of existence and his unchangeable identity is the provider of all the manifestations of life, including birth and death. To discover this essential center of self, Shah Maghsoud refers to his *'uqdah-i hayati* (locus of life), as a doorway to understanding what lies beyond the relativity of this world; a human being must find this divine identity in the third point of the heart, he says, where the worlds of the infinite and transient meet.[65] The physical body will undergo constant change and finally die. Elements return to their origin, and the complex wholeness of a system once called a "person" will disappear into the realm of non-visibility. If one permits oneself to be dissolved into the masses of nature, then he will be dissolved. If he finds a way to relate himself to the greater universe and truly understands that relationship, then he will ascend himself to a higher level of nature. And it is through understanding that higher universe that one may understand the absoluteness of his own self, the "I" of the universe.

· THE HUMAN UNIVERSE ·

Particles are like numbers, Shah Maghsoud writes, apparently limited but in reality unlimited. Nothing in the universe differs, essentially or outwardly, from the core principles, fundamental systems and order, and the wisdom of the universe. Particles when limited do not possess generality but in the infinity they are universal.[66]

---

[64] Quoted in Maurice Maeterlinck, *The Great Secret*, trans Bernard Miall (London: Methuen & Co. LTD, 1922) 73.

[65] For more information on Shah Maghsoud's *'uqdeh-e-hayati*, please see his *Payam-i dil*, translated by Nahid Angha as *A Meditation: Payam-i dil* (California: IAS Publications, 1991); Nahid Angha, *Shah Maghsoud: Life and Legacy* (California: International Association of Sufism, 2021) 115-137.

[66] Shah Maghsoud, *Padidihay-i fikr*, 28.

Experimental scientists tell us that things are made of waves or of the double qualities of wave (energy) and matter (density). Heat, light, sound, and so on, are all waves. What make them different are their frequencies, conditions, and relationships to the space. Now, just imagine that when science tells us that light is the wave of motion, or even separated particles forming a line, explanation is much different from what we *see* and *perceive*; what we see and perceive is neither the wave nor particles, but colors and light. This logic can be extended to everything that we perceive. With our laboratory equipment we are capable of more accurate understanding, but what is measured is only in the domain of our own confined universe. We understand only those rules that are harmonious with our nature. Our *time-dimension* cannot be understood other than in the dimension of space yet existence remains as it is: abstract, eternal, and infinite (we cannot say otherwise, because we do not know). So is there any *reality* within my being that is unchanging so it can understand that *reality*? Am I the absolute Self, an "I-ness" that remains the very core of my finite being? Do I have the means to understand *that* reality within the limitation of *this* corporeal being?

Shah Maghsoud suggests that while any confinement is limited but its meaning is not. To him, relativity, distance, limit, sense and so forth are like shadows presenting themselves as authentic; consuming us by their explanations of the ancient and infinite reality. However we are to remember that any "name" presents a limited understanding of a "meaning." What illuminates us is *life*, the absoluteness of life, the divine light that is hidden and entrusted to the very heart of every cell.[67] He indicates that frameworks and structures that we learn over time become the foundations of our perceptions and understanding. But like language, they are "frames" of space/time dimensions; they become veils over our understanding of the abstract nature of ultimate meaning. It is important to be conscious that the words we use do not become a mental prison, a confinement that we cannot break through. Then, if we consider the limitation of our tools of communication (i.e., language and so forth), we cannot be assured that the physical world is all that exists, or remain unaware of what may lie beyond our own

---

[67] Excerpts from Shah Maghsoud, *Hamaseh-i-hayat*, 4-5.

physical condition, and mistakenly conclude that the "beyond" does not exist. Our language-bound narratives of the complexity of the universe and cosmos hinder us from realizing what lies beneath and beyond the surface. Shah Maghsoud often gave the example of understanding the "I," which has a great complexity, beyond definitions. No one understands the "I," he says, except the "I" itself, and anything other than "I" is "other." The reality of a "thing" or a "being" lies within its own truth, and such a truth is an abstract essence that accompanies the "I" in its infinite and eternal journey. It is the core knowledge of the image, he says, that gives birth to the image; and thus an image is a journey of its own essential knowledge. This is not a travelling "away" but presenting the manifestation of a perfect and inherent calculation of the core knowledge.[68] So he asks: Is there an essence to this existence that creation is a living proof of its presence? Is there any reality other than what is apparent; and is a human being just a corporeality whirling in the whirlpool of time and space?

As long as anything *is*, it falls within the universal rule of being; our humanly limited possibilities of sense perceptions do not permit us to know the facts of existence; and *this* does not mean that there is no reality or fact to the existence. As our eyes cannot perceive sound waves, our minds cannot perceive the sublimity of eternity, the inherent knowledge within. Our philosophical theories, even though they have opened many doors toward understanding, will not open the door to understanding the boundless universe within the very essence of the human being: a human being who is in fact a confined universe carrying with himself the absolute knowledge. No theory will remain immortal. Every principle will be reviewed in its proper time. Yet the changeless and ageless infinite rules of existence will remain; they will surround the whole being from atom to galaxy, from matter to anti-matter, to wave to all those laws that we do not yet know or will never know. They rule by their perfect justice and balance. We, as this total being, will carry the abstract and justify the rule of universal unity. We, as the atom, carry the abstract, but will obey the rule and cooperate with our equals as we live and perceive within our boundaries.

So can we pierce through the veil of appearance, dimension, language,

---

[68] Nahid Angha, *Shah Maghsoud: Life and Legacy*, 176.

and touch the essence and meaning that they manifest? Can we understand the meaning of the Absolute, so we understand how the Abstract discloses itself in us, in every living being? Is a human being a non-repeating disclosure of his own Reality? Shah Maghsoud explains the concept in the metaphor of a raindrop and the ocean: a raindrop comes from the ocean, yet it is limited and bound to dimensions until it is dissolved in the ocean/water, to its essence. Thus a raindrop carries within itself the very essence of its own creation: water. It is a raindrop in its confinement and it is the ocean in its timelessness.[69]

Thus "we cannot overlook the possibility that within every cell there is an inherited knowledge, an essential core. This does not mean that there is an Infinite Absolute and a finite human, and that the two are separate and exist in duality; rather the Infinite presents itself as finite in order to be perceptible by the finite human being. Thus, the "I" of a human being becomes a dependable vehicle through which it can understand the Absolute. [...] And in a most eloquent language, Shah Maghsoud states that every cell of the universe, every rotating galaxy takes part in this journey of travelling through dimensions and directions; every breath participates in the spin in the pool of transformations. The infinite eternal leads galaxies to an endless journey, where particles rotate and waves reflect travelling in a circular journey presenting the Absolute core of being."[70]

So, the question remains: is there an intellectual center within the corporeal construct of the human system that understands this reality if not our mental faculties? To answer this question Shah Maghsoud refers to his notion of the locus of life: *'uqdah-i hayati* and writes about the electromagnetic centers of the human system.

· MAGNETIC CENTERS OF THE HUMAN SYSTEM ·

As the sound waves are spread into space by set computations so the susceptible recipient, according to its capacity and energy, receives and records them, so are the effects of human beings' thoughts; they,

---

[69] Ibid. 154.
[70] Ibid. 156.

too, will surely search and find—without time limitation—its suitable receivers within this boundless existence.[71]

With these words, Shah Maghsoud opens a door to an expanded understanding of the human universe; where the eternal and transient meet; the infinite is portrayed in the finite; the Absolute manifests itself in the domains of change; and the domain of change has the possibility to realize its Absoluteness: the hidden treasure that longs to be known, so it manifests itself in confinements so it will be known through its manifestations.[72] In his writings, Shah Maghsoud introduces such center, within the heart, that holds the light, energy and the certainty of the sacred knowledge and he calls this center the locus of life: *'uqdah-i hayati*.

In his *Padidihay-i fikr*, Shah Maghsoud refers to the emergence of the earth in its orbit to begin to nurture life. He also refers to the Earth's centers of electromagnetic energy and their cooperation with all the known and unknown energies of the universe. Indeed, we know, the Earth does not exist as a static object but rather through the continued synergy and influence of the energies of the cosmos. Likewise, the living organism exists as a continuous process, continuing only insofar as the balance between the twin powers of survival and destruction continues. Should the balance be lost, or one power overcomes the other, the manifestations of life would not hold the same appearance and existence as they do now.

If we review the formation of our galaxy as accurately as science has described it, we realize that we know little about the movement of this formation but an assumption of the first moment after the formation of what we call our universe. Science, in the twenty-first century, tells us that the first moment, after the formation, the universe suddenly appears on the face of existence as enormous explosions of force. The gas, cosmic dust, and electromagnetic systems surrounding this creation resonated into complex waves. With this radiant fireball, rapidly expanding, acting as a huge center of magnetic waves, the universe began. Then, it began

---

[71] Nahid Angha, trans. *Manifestations of Thought*, Introduction, 3.

[72] Related to the *hadith* of the Prophet: I (Allah/God) was a hidden treasure, I loved to be known so I created the creation so I would be known through my creations.

to fall into its place and dimensions, hand in hand, appeared on the steps of existence. No one knows how long ago our universe was created and formed, but fourteen billion years or so is a figure often given by scientists. They assume that after this huge explosion of so-called the Big Bang, a chaotic dance of gas, dust, electro and magnetic waves appeared, followed by a gradual transformation of inchoate force into the forms of energy and matter that form the substance of what we call our universe. This, at least, is the current view of science and my understanding of it, though it is based on assumptions that may very well be revised in the future. What we know about creation is what we can perceive through our speculations shaped by our perceptions. No matter how minutely they observe all this creation, perceptions are speculations, nonetheless. The universe does not need to pay heed to our expectations nor perform in accordance with them. Instead of relying on preconceived ideas about the world, we need to not only understand our limitations, admit what we do not know or mistakenly think we know, but also set aside our expectations and become more aware of our world both within and without.

Science tells us that galaxies are composed of gases and stars, emptiness and dust, and probably of more unknown or undetected compositions. There are hundreds of billions of stars in each galaxy, and there are some hundred billion galaxies.[73] Such a number leads any intelligent human being to wonder, "What is my position in the depth of such a huge existence? Can I really understand what lies within and without?"

We learn that the Milky Way, which contains over "400 billion stars of all sorts moving with a complex and orderly grace,"[74] is one of the many galaxies that we know of today. There, on its outskirts near the edge, is our solar system. There are possibly millions of suns with planets revolving about them in our galaxy, each of them searching for eternity and life. Where in this immensity does this immense intellect reside, if not in every particle?

When we look to the heavens at night, we see stars of different colors twinkling at us like signals in an undecipherable code letting us know that they, too, are living. "Some shine with constant brightness; others

---

[73] See Carl Sagan, *Cosmos* (New York: Random House, 1980) 6-7.
[74] Ibid. 10.

flicker uncertainly or blink with an unfaltering rhythm."[75] A telescope can discern blue, red, and yellow stars and even stars that shine with light beyond the spectrum of visible light. These colorful presentations of stars, each signifying an "age," remind us of the light-color-energies, introduced by Sufi masters, that an individual may experience during his or her meditation, signifying the depth of his or her concentration of energies. We learn that "[b]lue stars are hot and young; yellow stars, conventional and middle-aged; red stars are often elderly and dying; and small white or black stars are in their final throes of death."[76] Sounds so familiar of an inclusiveness of the birth and death of all that exists. In every second of time, the universe witnesses the births and deaths of confines, ascending the ladder to perfection.

Since the beginning of time, the absoluteness of life has been infused in all that exists—planets and stars, and all that claim life. Our tiny planet of Earth was born, and life on Earth began to emerge as we, or any entity, the microcosms, were born from the beautiful colorful living macrocosms, with all the same substances that have been giving birth to our universe. No one can overestimate the role that electro and magnetic energies and cosmic dust have played in the birth of the human being. We are the children of space and time. We inherit the life's intellect that founded the universe. We are the universe. Can we study the human being and forget his origin, the cosmic waves and energies? Are there many different universes, of different origins, or ultimately a unity? Isn't it true that "Every now and then a passing star gives a tiny gravitational tug, and one of the obligingly careens into the inner solar system, [t]here the Sun heats it, the ice is vaporized, and a lovely cometary tail develops"[77] and death opens the door for the emergence of life? If those gravitational tugs exist and travel into the "inner solar system," then where do we experience those "gravitational tugs" within the human system, where is that attractive energy that pulls you and I?

The formation of any being is not separable from the vast ocean of space, and all are in connection to the celestial and ultra-celestial waves. Any being is in an encompassing connection and relation to the rest

---

[75] Ibid. 10.
[76] Ibid. 10.
[77] Ibid. 11.

of existence. Nothing is wholly separated from any other thing, even though the human is lonely in his being.

Shah Maghsoud mentions that from the very beginning as Earth settled down into its balanced orbit, and began to represent life as it is for us, its electromagnetic energies have been in constant connection and relation with all the eternal energies in the existence. And the human being, who is a connecting link between the seen and unseen, is the recipient of both active and receptive energies of this infinite and eternal environment. So it is of utmost importance that we discover the facts of these unknown past and future realities of the present time; understanding these realities will help us to understand the notions of birth and death.

The exchange and transmission of electro and magnetic wave energies (among others), according to Shah Maghsoud, leads the galaxies, the cosmos, the wandering stars, and every particle including the human being to their destinations; they are the transmitter of life. The exchange and transmission of these energies are from storages, capacitors and centers; and thus every element, in this boundless universe, is a potential sender and receiver of energies, including the human being.

Let us take the hydrogen molecule as an example for our investigation. So Shah Maghsoud asks, "How accurately can we measure all the energies, active and receptive, of this vital molecule? Has not this molecule in its celestial and cosmic journey become the recipient of solar and cosmic waves and energies? Is not this molecule an essential substratum in the formation of life and our living? Is not the transference of energies one of the qualities of this molecule, since water is one of the strongest substances in transferring electromagnetic waves? How then can we overlook this simple equation in our own life, and forget that we, too, are powerful centers of electromagnetic waves as well as the recipient of these waves?"[78] He answers these questions through elaborated explanations emphasizing the importance of paying attention to the principles and the universality of the forces in the cosmos and their relation to the earth and consequently to the human being in order to understand the totality of the human being and its strength. We may only see a body, he advises, while forgetting the forces and the

---

[78] For more information see *Tib-i sunnati*, 57.

energies within it. If science learns more about the energies and the reactions of the environmental waves and their relations to the cells and existing molecules, it will be able to accomplish more than it now does. We cannot purport to present a complete understanding or description of a being independent from the boundless ocean of space and what lies beyond space, without considering all the actions, reactions, and nature of the existing energies and forces.

Shah Maghsoud explains that the complex systems of action, reaction, and cooperation between the electromagnetic forces and energies give birth to an organism. Their domain reaches beyond the orbit of Earth and they follow a harmonious balance as the principle governing the cosmos and its orbits. The magnetic waves and their effects are distributed from the magnetic centers and capacitors. As these systems exist within the orbit of Earth, they exist as well within every particle of the earth, all of which follow the rules of harmony and balance. These same laws cover the domain of magnetic actions and reactions of the universe. The individual human being, as one of the particles of the earth, possesses, without any doubt, the same electromagnetic energies and forces that govern the earth, its orbit and beyond. A being, a particle, or an organism is the recipient, the transferee, and the repository of these energies and forces. If the molecules of hydrogen and oxygen in their combined form as water transfer electricity, why not also the human being, who is mostly composed of water? We may be able to see the transference of energy in the molecule of hydrogen and yet be unable to see the same process in more complex substances, such as metals and so forth. If the complexity of other molecules and elements does not permit us to observe more precisely, it is not because such processes of the transference of energy do not exist but merely because we do not see! Yet the neurologist's model of the brain is based upon a system of chemical reactions producing electrical impulses that travel through the nerves and through them to the entire body.[79]

Apart from their interest from scientists of the future, the magnetic centers of the human body have already been the subject of investigations, especially for the schools of spirituality. The reason lies in the fact that proper concentration within and on any one of

---

[79] For more information see *Negāh*, Chapter Seven.

these centers will end in fruitful metaphysical and spiritual under-standing. Thus, the task of correctly distinguishing these centers, their locations in the body, and their capability is of great importance for anyone who seeks to understand the sacred knowledge, knowledge beyond the ordinary.

Shah Maghsoud undertook the broadest discussion of thirteen magnetic centers of the human body and their relationships and com-munications with the magnetic rays in the universe in his writings. These centers or capacitors absorb energies and make them suitable for the human being by transforming the energies into forms of mag-netism as well as other substances necessary to the human body. These delicate and fine centers are active as well as passive, they are effective as well as affected. Science must give more credit, he suggests, to the world of human energy in order to understand the human being as a complete entity.

Among the most important of these centers is what he calls the locus of life: *'uqdah-i hayati*. He suggests that these thirteen electromagnetic centers in the human system, including the heart, are in direct rela-tionship with the electromagnetic forces of the cosmos, function as the secondary repositories of life energies, and receive and transform the electromagnetic energies of the extended universe into harmonious, useful energies/materials suitable for human systems (just as current electrical waves are transmitted from central power sources to second-ary centers through cables and wires that interface with the secondary receiver). When one of these centers experiences a failure (and dys-function), he mentions, the entire nervous and magnetic centers of the human system notice the effect. Understanding these centers helps a human being to learn about the medium between the human physical body and one's finer self. I have addressed some of these theories, in more detail, in other commentaries on Shah Maghsoud's doctrines.

The "locus of life," Shah Maghsoud mentions, is located in the third point upper right section of the heart. Its magnetic particles are nourished by sunlight; its wave lines are horizontal and cross the nerve lines of the nervous system. This center is the agent of much essential learning in life. One such learning is understanding the notion of love, an energy, a gravitational force, that connects the particles of being together, and its function is continuous and highly organized, and it may be comparable to the meaning of life that brings essential being into apparent shapes and forms.

We have learned that among the most important human organs that produce electromagnetism are the brain and heart. However, it seems that the heart is not only the life-giving organ, but it also produces the greatest electromagnetic field in the body. But where is this "third point" that Shah Maghsoud has called the locus of life, the life-giving center, the most important center of electromagnetic field in the human body? Looking at the scientific studies to understand more about the existence and function of such a "locus" within the heart, we learn that, "In the upper part of the right atrium of the heart is a specialized bundle of neurons known as the sinoatrial node (SA node). The electrical impulse from the SA node triggers a sequence of electrical events in the heart to control the orderly sequence of muscle contractions that pump the blood out of the heart"[80] "The electrical stimulus travels down through the conduction pathways and causes the heart's ventricles to contract and pump out blood."[81] And we learn that the "beating of the heart" announcing the travel of these electrical waves to sustain life is fundamental in our survival, and our life depends on those "pumping outs" of the oxygenated blood to sustain our corporeal life. Shah Maghsoud indicates that understanding this locus helps us to step beyond the survival of our corporeality.

Is Shah Maghsoud's notion of *'uqdah-i hayati* a reference to the importance of the sinoatrial node, a *self-firing*[82] node in the human heart that not only sets the rhythm of life through heartbeat but also generates electrical stimulus? He does not mention this node by name but his concept of such a node directs us to the same notion, to this locus that, perhaps, plays the most significant role in human health and

[80] See The Sinoatrial Node: The Body's Natural Pacemaker, http://hyperphysics. phy-astr.gsu.edu/hbase/Biology/sanode.html

[81] For more information see The heart's electrical system: https://www.hopkins-medicine.org/health/conditions-and-diseases/anatomy-and-function-of-the-hearts-electrical-system.

[82] "While it is the norm for nerve cells that they require a stimulus to fire, the SA node can be considered to be "self-firing". It repetitively goes through a depolarizing discharge and then repolarizes to fire again." http://hyperphysics.phy-astr.gsu.edu/hbase/Biology/sanode.html

life expectancy; and its dysfunction seems to perhaps cause the death of the human system.

To understand the human universe in its totality, Shah Maghsoud focuses on the wholeness of the human being, body and soul, mind and heart in his philosophical, scientific and metaphysical approach. He indicates that if we are to understand the realms beyond our immediate interaction with nature, we are to learn and pay more attention to the cosmic energies, electromagnetic forces and their relationship with the human system. He suggests that our understanding of these centers within the corporeality of the human system, especially the center within the heart, is of great urgency; especially since the heart has significant effects on the human organism and its longevity. Thus, it is necessary, he advises, that we understand and learn about the energy forces and electromagnetic qualities of cells, their relationship and connections to their surroundings, as well as to the universe and cosmic-wave-energies if we are to offer a safe and better life to humanity.[83] Such understanding is of great significance since we have learned that our body does, in fact, generates electrical activity through our cells, and this, in reality, makes us a magnetic field, and in relationship with all cosmic energies, seen and unseen, known and unknown.

Shah Maghsoud has written through a great elaboration explaining the role of each one of the magnetic centers of the human system; as they all are important to the survival of the body. For example, he refers to a center located in the forehead, between the two eye-bows, that will cause a human being to develop insight; he refers to the last disc in the spinal cord as one of the most important vital centers of the human system, and the center located in the soft spot in the skull as a vital receiver of the cosmic energies, and the grey surface of the brain, and more. He suggests that our system is a great energy force connected through lines of the nervous system and cells, and in relationship with the sun's magnetic rays as well as the energy waves of the ultimate space. Therefore, if our studies advance and science comes to a better realization of the human body as a whole, many of our illnesses can possibly be cured through the safe usage of sunlight.

Shah Maghsoud also gives a meditative practice in his *Payam-i dil*,

---

[83] For more information on this subject see *Shah Maghsoud: Life and Legacy.*

in this regards; and in a most beautiful language of imagery and metaphors, he tells us how these wave energies will lead us to a greater understanding, and writes:

> When the energies of your senses gather and reach the house of your heart and wish not to turn back, you will find your "self," and when your being is nourished by the "locus of life," you will see the illuminating face of your "self" [....].[84] Illusions gather together and scatter asunder in different forms. The human being takes them on a journey but does not travel with them [....]. The eternal essence exists in the depths and surfaces of all beings and will not disappear. But while manifested beings always gather and scatter, the wholeness of existence is neither increased nor decreased by their gatherings and scatterings [....]. This infinite extension from a particle to the whole, from atom to the universe is but constant births that fall into dispersion and death. The appearance of life is a presentation of the great expansions and condensations, but the truth and the essence of life is the eternal and immortal originality.[85]

Shah Maghsoud tells us that the "locus of life" is the connecting point between the two worlds of heaviness (condensed matter/physical body) and refinement (subtle light/spiritual body). Of these two realms, one leads toward infinity and the other toward finitude. The human being must find his divine identity where these two worlds meet in the twilight state between sleep and waking;[86] where the world of conscious life faces the world of sleeping death, the first pulls toward eternity and infinity while the second pushes toward the depth of transience.[87]

The principle of harmony permeates all that exists or at least within our universe—it leads the attractive and attracted forces to

---

[84] *A Meditation*, 10.

[85] Ibid. 11.

[86] Ibn ʿArabi also refers to this state of waking and sleep where one may experience a mystical enlightenment. See Claude Addas, *Quest for the Red Sulphur: The Life of Ibn ʿArabi* (Cambridge: The Islamic Texts Society: Golden Palm Series, 1993) 290.

[87] For more information see *A Meditation*.

their destinations. Then, possibly, the key to unveiling the realm of the infinite is to understand the heart of the indivisible finite world, and, to understand that connecting point of "togetherness," unity. Since everything in existence follows the principle of harmony, then a human being is capable to gather and concentrate his energies, in a central fixed point of reference, or as Shah Maghsoud suggests on the heart's locus of life, and in creating such forces of energies and electromagnetic environment around himself, he becomes attune to favorable wavelength to receive his share of this magnificent infinite Being, a share that may help him to surpass the limitation of the confinements of his present corporeality to become infinite and be re-absorbed into his original home: eternity.

· EPILOGUE ·

Within the realm of nature's dictations and everlasting hope to understand the infinite, we have to find a common ground where these two realities—the world of finite and the realm of infinite—meet.

Life is the interaction between hidden and apparent forces, and the human being is constantly receiving and distributing those energies. Since the rules and laws of harmony and cooperation are among the most effective laws governing the universe, a human being receives only those waves for which he or she is attuned to receive. The essential law of harmony is timeless and universal; is free from the confines of dimensions; it permeates every particle of seen and the unseen, all of that which exists. In this magnificent cycle of creation, we take our part as individuals and each experience our surroundings in the limitation of our individuation. Our perceptions set us apart from the whole sum of the universe, yet every manifestation of existence has its core in that stable and unchanging eternal essence; its essential knowledge.

In this awesome stage of creation, we each take a part and select our affairs and thus experience what is most suited to our perceptions and understanding. In such isolation, we may forget that the essence of Unity permeates the domain of nature, and it is the hand of harmony that brings the heart of the attracted in union with the heart of that which attracts. It is important to understand that any bridge will lead us to a destination, and our destination becomes our God, our pole. Whatever attracts us become our attracted pole, our inspiration, and our goal. Limitation leads to confinements, and freedom from finite leads to eternal; whatever is born will die, and whatever dies belongs to the state of change. However, the absolute, the core of that which manifests, is eternal, is the knowledge that has journeyed with its manifestations throughout the immense journey of becoming, as it leads the wandering stars to their destination it also leads the heart to the very essence of life, free from finite and transient.

BIBLIOGRAPHY

A Pale Blue Dot. https://www.planetary.org/worlds/pale-blue-dot

Addas, Claude. *Quest for the Red Sulphur: The Life of Ibn 'Arabi*. Cambridge: The Islamic Texts Society: Golden Palm Series, 1993.

Angha, Nahid. *Negāh: Tahshi'-i-bar Padidihay-i fikr*. Tehran, Maktab-i-tariqat-Uwaiysi-Shah Maghsoudi Series, 1979.

———. *Shah Maghsoud: Life and Legacy*. San Rafael, California: International Association of Sufism Publications, 2021.

Angha, Nahid, trans. *A Meditation: Payam-i dil*. California: International Association of Sufism Publications, 1991.

———. *Manifestations of Thought*. San Rafael, California: Educational Testing & Research Institute Publications, 1980.

———. *Nirvan*. California: International Association of Sufism, 2021; first edition 1991.

———. *Psalms of Gods: Avaz-i-khudayan*. California: IAS Publications, 1991.

Angha, Shah Maghsoud Sadiq. *Zavaya-yi makhfi hayati*. Tehran: Amin Publications, 1975.

———. *Hamaseh-i-hayat*. Tehran: Amin Publications, 1974.

———. *Hidden Angles of Life*. Pomona, California: Multidisciplinary Publications, 1975.

———. *Nirvan, Avaz-i-khudayan, Payam-i-dil, Padidihay-i fikr*. Tehran: Amin Publications, 1963.

Ariew, Roger. *Rene Descartes: Philosophical Essays and Correspondence*. Indianapolis: Hackett Publishing Company, Inc., 2000.

Astore, Rocco A. "Examining Free-Will Through Spinoza and Descartes." *Inquiries: Philosophy*, Vol. 8, No. 02, 2016.

Atkins, Peter. *The Laws of Thermodynamics*. Oxford: Oxford University Press, 2010.

Aurelius, Marcus. *Meditations.* Translated by Gregory Hays. New York: Modern Library, 2003.

Bergson, Henri. *Creative Evolution.* New York: Henry Holt and Company, 1911.

Berryman, Sylvia. "Democritus." *The Stanford Encyclopedia of Philosophy* (Winter 2016 Edition), Edward N. Zalta (ed.), URL = https://plato.stanford.edu/archives/win2016/entries/democritus/

Bonazzi, Mauro. "Protagoras." *The Stanford Encyclopedia of Philosophy* (Fall 2020 Edition), Edward N. Zalta (ed.), URL=https://plato.stanford.edu/archives/fall2020/entries/protagoras/

Breazeale, Dan. "Johann Gottlieb Fichte." *The Stanford Encyclopedia of Philosophy* (Summer 2018 Edition), Edward N. Zalta (ed.), URL = https://plato.stanford.edu/archives/sum2018/entries/johann-fichte

Brown, Robin Gordon and James Ladyman. *Materialism: A Historical and Philosophical Inquiry.* New York: Taylor&Francis, 2019.

Cahan, David. Ed. *Hermann von Helmholtz and the Foundations of Nineteenth-Century Science.* Berkeley: University of California Press, 1993.

Clarke, Desmond. *Descartes' Philosophy of Science.* Manchester: Manchester University Press, 1982.

Crowell, Steven. "Existentialism." *The Stanford Encyclopedia of Philosophy* (Summer 2020 Edition), Edward N. Zalta (ed.), URL= https://plato.stanford.edu/archives/sum2020/entries/existentialism/

Descartes, René. *Discourse on Method and Related Writings.* Translated by R. Ariew. New York: Penguin, 1993.

———. *Discourse on Method and Related Writings.* Translated by Desmond Clarke. New York: Penguin, 1993.

———. *Discourse on Method.* Translated by Ian Maclean. New York: Oxford University Press, 2008.

———. *Principles of Philosophy.* Translated by Valentine Rodger Miller and Reese P. Miller. Netherlands: Springer, 2012.

Di Liscia, Daniel A. "Johannes Kepler." *The Stanford Encyclopedia of Philosophy* (Fall 2019 Edition), Edward N. Zalta (ed.), URL = https://plato.stanford.edu/archives/fall2019/entries/kepler/

First Law of Thermodynamics. https://www.toppr.com/guides/physics/thermodynamics/first-law-of-thermodynamics/

Bibliography

Flammarion, Camille. *Death and its Mystery: Before Death*. Volume I. Translated by E. S. Brooks. Charleston, South Carolina: Nabu Press, 2010.

Fox, Sidney W. "Aleksandr Oparin, Russian biochemist." *Encyclopedia Britannica* (nd).

Gerber, Daniel. *Descartes' Metaphysical Physics*. Chicago: University of Chicago Press, 1992.

Goldstein, Catherine, Norbert Schappacher and Joachim Schwermer. Edited. *The Shaping of Arithmetic after C.F. Gauss's Disquisitiones Arithmeticae*. New York: Springer, 2007.

Hatfield, Gary. "René Descartes." *The Stanford Encyclopedia of Philosophy* (Summer 2018 Edition), Edward N. Zalta (ed.), URL = <https://plato.stanford.edu/archives/sum2018/entries/descartes/>.

Hegel, Georg Wilhelm Friedrich. *The Phenomenology of the Spirit*. Translated by Terry Pinkard. New York: Cambridge University Press, 2018.

———. *The Philosophy of History*. New York: Dover, 1956.

Hipschman, Ron. *Exploratorium*. "Your Weight on Other Worlds." https://www.exploratorium.edu/ronh/weight/.

Hospers, John. https://depthome.sunysuffolk.edu/Selden/Philosophy/SE/handouts/Hospers.pdf, 357.

———. "What Means This Freedom?" *Determination and Freedom in the Age of Modern Science*. Edited by in Sidney Hook. New York: SUNY Press, 1958.

Janiak, Andrew. "Newton's Philosophy." *The Stanford Encyclopedia of Philosophy* (Winter 2019 Edition), Edward N. Zalta (ed.), URL = https://plato.stanford.edu/archives/win2019/entries/newton-philosophy/

Jeans, James. *The Dynamical Theory of Gases*. Cambridge: Cambridge University Press, 1925.

Jennie, "The Poet's Testament" George Santayana, 2015: https://wordsfortheyear.com/2015/04/01/the-poets-testament-by-george-santayana/

Jervis-Smith, Frederick John. *Evangelista Torricelli*. Oxford: Oxford University Press, 1908.

Kant, Immanuel. *Observations on the Feeling of the Beautiful and Sublime*. Translated by John T. Goldthwait. Berkeley: University of California Press, 1960.

Leibniz, G.W. *New Essays on Human Understanding*. Translated by Peter Remnant and Jonathan Bennett. United Kingdom: Cambridge University Press, 1996.

Lesher, James. "Xenophanes." *The Stanford Encyclopedia of Philosophy* (Summer 2021 Edition), Edward N. Zalta (ed.), URL=https://plato.stanford.edu/archives/sum2019/entries/xenophanes/.

Levy, Lior. "Reflection, Memory and Selfhood in Jean-Paul Sartre's Early Philosophy." *Sartre Studies International*, Berghahn Books, Vol. 19, No. 2.

Lex Newman, "Descartes' Epistemology." *The Stanford Encyclopedia of Philosophy* (Spring 2019 Edition), Edward N. Zalta (ed.), URL=https://plato.stanford.edu/archives/spr2019/entries/descartes-epistemology/

Look, Brandon C. "Gottfried Wilhelm Leibniz." *The Stanford Encyclopedia of Philosophy* (Spring 2020 Edition), Edward N. Zalta (ed.), URL=https://plato.stanford.edu/archives/spr2020/entries/libniz/

Machamer, Peter and David Marshall Miller. "Galileo Galilei." *The Stanford Encyclopedia of Philosophy* (Summer 2021 Edition) Edward N. Zalta (ed.), URL=https://plato.stanford.edu/archives/sum2021/entries/galileo/

Maeterlinck, Maurice. *The Great Secret*. Translated by Bernard Miall. New York: The Century Company, 1922.

———. *Wisdom and Destiny*. Translated by Alfred Sutro. London: George Allen, Ruskin House, mdcccxcviii, 1898.

Mark, Joshua J. "Protagoras." *The Ancient History Encyclopedia*, 2009.

Mates, Benson. *The Philosophy of Leibniz*. Oxford: Oxford University Press, 1986.

McCormick, Matt. "Immanuel Kant: Metaphysics." *The Internet Encyclopedia of Philosophy*, nd. URL=https://iep.utm.edu/kantmeta/

Mesmer, Franz. Brain, *Mind and Medicine: Essays in Eighteenth-Century Neuroscience*. Edited by C.U.M. Smith, Harry Whitaker and Stanley Finger. New York: Springer, 2007.

Millgram, Elijah. *John Stuart Mill and the Meaning of Life*. Oxford: Oxford University Press, 2019.

Nadler, Steven. "Baruch Spinoza." *The Stanford Encyclopedia of Philosophy* (summer 2020 Edition), Edward N. Zalta (ed.), URL=https://plato.stanford.edu/archives/sum2020/entries/spinoza/

Newman, Lex. "Descartes' Epistemology." *The Stanford Encyclopedia of Philosophy* (Spring 2019 Edition), Edward N. Zalta (ed.), URL=https://plato.stanford.edu/archives/spr2019/entries/descartes-epistemology/

Newton, Isaac. *Opticks: Or A Treatise of the Reflections, Refractions, Inflections, and Colours of Light*, 4th edition. Gale ECCO, Print Editions, 2018.

———. *The Principia: Mathematical Principles of Natural Philosophy* Translated by I. Bernard Cohen and Anne Whitman. Berkeley: University of California Press, 1999.

Nolan, Lawrence. "Descartes, Ontological Argument." *The Stanford Encyclopedia of Philosophy* (Spring 2021 Edition) Edward N. Zalta (ed.), URL=http://plato.stanford.edu/archives/spr2021/entries/descartes-ontological/

———. "Malebranche's Theory of Ideas and Vision in God." *The Stanford Encyclopedia of Philosophy* (Spring 2022 Edition), Edward N. Zalta (ed.), URL=https://plato.stanford.edu/archives/spr2022/entries/malebrache-idea/

Oparin, Alexander. *The Origin of Life on Earth*. New York: Dover Publications, 1965.

Pearson, Keith Ansell and John Mullarkey, edited. *Henry Bergson Key Writings*. New York: Continuum, 2002.

Plato. *The Last Days of Socrates*. Translated by Christopher Rowe. New York: Penguin, 2010.

Redding, Paul. "Georg Wilhelm Friedrich Hegel." *The Stanford Encyclopedia of Philosophy* (Winter 2020 Edition), Edward N. Zalta (ed.), URL = https://plato.stanford.edu/archives/win2020/entries/hegel/

Rescher, Nicholas. *On Leibniz*. Pittsburgh: University of Pittsburgh Press, 2013.

Rhine, J.B. *Extra-Sensory Perception*. Boston: B. Humphries, 1964.

Rohlf, Michael . "Immanuel Kant." *Stanford Encyclopedia of Philosophy* (Fall 2020 Edition), Edward N. Zalta (ed.), URL= https://plato.stanford.edu/archives/fall2020/entries/kant/

Ryan, John, K. Translator. *The Confessions of St. Augustine*. New York: Random House, 1960.

Saatkamp, Herman and Martin Coleman. "George Santayana." *The Stanford Encyclopedia of Philosophy* (Fall 2020 Edition), Edward N. Zalta (ed.), URL= https://plato.stanford.edu/archives/fall2020/entries/santayana/

Sacred Texts: Christianity Angelus Silesius, *VIII: TIME AND ETERNITY*: https://www.sacred-texts.com/chr/sil/scw/scw08.htm

Sagan, Carl. *Cosmos*. New York: Random House, 1980.

Santayana, George. *The Poet's Testament: Poems and Two Plays*. New York: Charles Scribner's Sons, 1953.

Sartre, Jean-Paul. *Being and Nothingness*. Translated by Hazel E. Barnes. Washington Square Press, 1993.

Schmaltz, Tad. "Nicolas Malebranche." *The Stanford Encyclopedia of Philosophy* (Winter 2017), Edward N. Zalta (ed.), URL=https://plato.stanford.edu/archive/win2017/entries/malenranche/

Shein, Noa. "Spinoza's Theory of Attributes." *The Stanford Encyclopedia of Philosophy* (Spring 2018 Edition), Edward N. Zalta (ed.), URL= https://plato.stanford.edu/archives/spr2018/entries/spinoza-attributes/

Smith, C.U.M., Harry Whitaker and Stanley Finger, Eds. *Brain, Mind and Medicine: Essays in Eighteenth-Century Neuroscience*. New York: Springer, 2007.

Spinoza, Benedict. *Ethics*, E. Curley, Ed. Princeton: Penguin Books, 1996.

Taylor, C.C.W. Translator. *The Atomists Leucippus and Democritus*. Toronto: University of Toronto Press, 1999.

Taylor, Michael W. Translator. *The Philosophy of Herbert Spencer*. New York: Continuum, 2007.

The heart's electrical system. https://www.hopkinsmedicine.org/health/conditions-and-diseases/anatomy-and-function-of-the-hearts-electrical-system.

The Physics of the Universe: Alexander Oparin. https://www.physicsoftheuniverse.com/scientists_oparin.html

The Sinoatrial Node: The Body's Natural Pacemaker. http://hyperphysics.phy-astr.gsu.edu/hbase/Biology/sanode.html

Troxell, Mary. "Arthur Schopenhauer." *The Internet Encyclopedia of Philosophy*, nd. https://iep.utm.edu/schopenh/

Watkins, Eric and Marius Stan. "Kant's Philosophy of Science." *The Stanford Encyclopedia of Philosophy* (Fall 2014 Edition), Edward N. Zalta (ed.), URL= https://plato.stanford.edu/archives/fall2014/entries/kant-science/

Wheeler, Michael. "God's Machines: Descartes on the Mechanization of Mind." *The Mechanical Mind in History*. Edited by Phil Husbands. Cambridge, Mass: MIT Press, 2008.

Wicks, Robert. "Arthur Schopenhauer." *The Stanford Encyclopedia of Philosophy* (Fall 2021 Edition), Edward N. Zalta (ed.), URL= https://plato.stanford.edu/archives/fall2021/entries/ schopenhauer/

Yezzi, Ron. Free Will and Determinism: Hard Determinism: https://sites.google.com/site/rythinkingtourspi2/harddeterminism.

———. *Philosophical Problems: God, Free Will, and Determinism*. Mankato: G. Bruno & Co. 1993.

INDEX

Absolute, 28, 32, 34, 40, 41, 42, 66, 72, 84, 85, 94, 95; -reality, 29
Abu al-Hassan Kharaqani, 34
Abu Sa'id Abul-Khayr, 34
Al-Rasa'il (Treatises), xvi
Amuli, Abul-Abass, 34
Angelus Silesius, 85
Apollo, 37
Atman, 90, 91
Avaz-i khudayan (Psalms of Gods), xv

beauty, 38; of nature, 55
Being, 33, 38, 42, 55, 64, 67, 78, 104; actuality of, 59; knowledge of 60; laws of, 69
Bergson, Henri, 10
Big Bang, 96
birth, 14, 40, 64, 82, 86, 97; and death, 40, 85, 86, 87, 89, 91, 97, 98, 103; before, 47, 86; second, 42
Brahma, 90, 91
Buddhism, 49

Cauchy, Augustin-Louis, 21
causality, 62; theory of, 58
cause: and effect, 30, 41, 47, 58, 59, 61, 62, 63, 67, 72; First, 63, 64, 67, 68
Chante: Jahan-i 'Arif (Chante: The Universe of the Knower), xv, 44
consciousness, 7, 12, 25, 55, 83
creation, 63, 64, 65, 74, 76, 90, 93, 95, 96, 104
Creator, 64, 65
death, 40, 85, 86, 87, 88, 89, 90, 97, 102; after, 86, 87, 89; and birth, 85, 86, 87, 89, 91, 98, 103

Delphi: oracle, 37; Temple, 89
Democritus, 24
Descartes, René, 4, 14, 40, 59, 65, 66
destiny, 13, 14, 32, 48, 50, 62, 64, 70, 72, 74, 77, 80, 82
Diwan-i ghazal (Book of Sonnet), xiii, xvi
DNA, 73, 75, 81, 82, 89
Duke of Brunswick, 19

electromagnetic: centers of the human system, 94, 100; cosmic forces, 100, 102; energy, 89, 95, 97, 98, 99, 100; field in the human body, 101; force, 61; waves, 17, 29, 96, 98
electromagnetism, 101
essence, 33, 62, 66, 72; absolute, 72; abstract, 66, 72, 90, 93; eternal, 90, 103, 104
eternity, 60, 76, 80, 85, 93, 103
ethics, 40, 68, 79
existence, 13, 24, 26, 27, 29, 33, 40, 41, 59, 64, 66, 67, 70, 71, 72, 80, 81, 82, 84, 85, 93, 103, 104
Existentialism, 69

Fichte, Johann, 49
Flammarion, Camille, 86
free will, 15, 26, 28, 62, 63, 64, 65, 67, 68, 69, 70, 71, 72

Galileo Galilei, 8, 20
Gauss, Johann Carl Friedrich, 19
God, xiv, 33, 37, 60, 63, 64, 67, 68, 105; God's will, 68
Group Theory, 21

115